RHS

The LITTLE BOOK of
SMALL-SPACE
Gardening

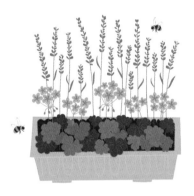

RHS The Little Book of Small-space Gardening

Author: Kay Maguire

First published in Great Britain in 2018 by Mitchell Beazley, an imprint of
Octopus Publishing Group Ltd
Carmelite House, 50 Victoria Embankment, London EC4Y 0DZ
www.octopusbooks.co.uk

An Hachette UK Company
www.hachette.co.uk

Published in association with the Royal Horticultural Society

ISBN: 978 1 78472 426 9

A CIP record of this book is available from the British Library

Set in Gill Sans, Madurai and Amatic

Printed and bound in China

Mitchell Beazley Publisher: Alison Starling

RHS Head of Editorial: Chris Young

RHS Publisher: Rae Spencer-Jones

Conceived, designed and produced by The Bright Press,
an imprint of The Quarto Group.
The Old Brewery, 6 Blundell Street,
London N7 9BH, United Kingdom
T (0) 20 7700 6700 F (0)20 7700 8066
www.QuartoKnows.com

Cover and book design: Clare Barber

Illustrations: Alyssa Peacock

RHS consultant editor: Simon Maughan

With thanks to Holly Farrell

The Royal Horticultural Society is the UK's leading gardening charity
dedicated to advancing horticulture and promoting good gardening. Its charitable work includes
providing expert advice and information, training the next generation of gardeners, creating hands-on
opportunities for children to grow plants and conducting research into plants, pests and
environmental issues affecting gardeners.
For more information visit www.rhs.org.uk or call 0845 130 4646.

MIX
Paper from
responsible sources
FSC® C008047

RHS

The LITTLE BOOK of
SMALL-SPACE
Gardening

EASY-GROW IDEAS FOR
BALCONIES, WINDOW BOXES
& OTHER OUTDOOR AREAS

KAY MAGUIRE

CONTENTS

INTRODUCTION

Gardening is, put simply, the act of growing plants. The available space does not determine whether or not you are a gardener. You may yearn for an acre of land somewhere, and yet you live in a flat in a city. Perhaps you only have room for a narrow box on a windowsill, or maybe you are lucky enough to have a little outside space in the form of a balcony. These spaces, though small, have the potential to be filled with the colour and vibrancy of plants, bringing you, and those around you, constant joy.

Plants are amazingly adaptable, and, wherever you live, there is something you can grow. For thousands of years, and all over the world, plants have been evolving and adapting to cope with all kinds of harsh conditions, which means that even the tiniest, dingiest, windiest balcony can support plants, and they will not only survive, but thrive.

The most unlikely spots can become a garden. Even though windowsills, walls, ledges, fire escapes, doorsteps and balconies can be more challenging places to grow than a traditional garden, it is still possible to transform them into thriving, productive growing spaces. They can be shrouded in shade, next to a noisy, busy road, exposed to rough winds or scorched by the sun. None of these situations are ideal, but nor are they impossible to overcome.

Look around and imagine everywhere and anywhere as potential growing space – every inch you have, every surface and wall, can support plants. If you're itching to get growing, don't let a lack of space or a seemingly unpromising site hold you back; chances are, there is more to it than meets the eye!

HOW TO USE THIS BOOK

This book is a practical guide to growing in some of the smallest and trickiest spaces, from windowsills to the urban balcony. With simple projects and clear advice, it is an inspirational book that can either be dipped into or read from cover to cover, depending on where and how you wish to garden.

CHAPTER 1 looks at the benefits of filling small spaces with plants, not only for us, but for the wildlife and broader environment around us. It also addresses the challenges that these tiny, often tricky spaces can present.

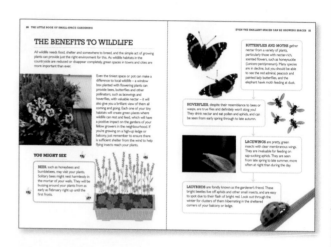

CHAPTER 2 covers the importance of growing the right plants in the right place. It explains how even the most challenging environments, from the shadiest terrace to the windiest balcony, can be beautiful, thriving growing spaces, as long as you choose the plants that can cope with your conditions.

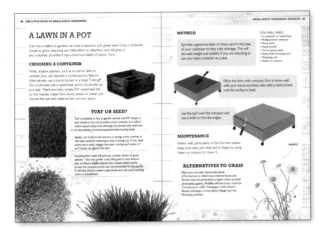

CHAPTER 3 consists of projects to get creative with, ranging from wildlife-friendly and edible pots, to containers that will thrive and overcome the tricky conditions found up high or in tiny spaces. Each project includes a list of plants and equipment, and clear steps on how to create it.

CHAPTER 4 is a practical guide, covering everything you need to know to keep your plants and small-space garden going, from the tools needed, to simple advice on good growing techniques, including planting, sowing, watering and feeding.

Finally, the book ends with a glossary, explaining technical terms, and a resources section including websites, books and other inspirational sources that will help you get going with your small-space garden.

Chapter 1

EVEN THE SMALLEST SPACES CAN BE GROWING SPACES

Plants can and will grow even in the tiniest of outdoor spaces; you only have to look at the weeds growing in paving cracks and on building ledges to appreciate their tenacity. Obviously, there is a big difference between a weedy front step and a welcoming, lush oasis: the trick is to use the plants that will best suit the conditions of your outdoor space to create the small garden of your dreams.

Just being able to see plants, even just a few pots, will lift your mood and delight your neighbours and visitors. Plants also provide valuable food and shelter for bees, butterflies and other wildlife. Planting a small-space garden can even be good for the local house prices: it's a win–win situation!

This chapter shows just how good a few plants in a small space can be. Overcoming challenges from wind, shade and drought is covered in depth, so that even the most cramped and dingy spaces can be transformed into a horticultural haven.

SMALL SPACE POSITIVES

Tiny gardens and small growing spaces crammed into, or eked out of, small spaces might have their challenges, but they also have their own unique advantages.

EASY TO MANAGE

Growing in a small space can be much easier than in a large garden. Soil can be limited or non-existent, but little raised beds, pots and containers need much less maintenance than bigger borders and great stretches of land. Having fewer plants requires less work and fewer resources, such as water and feed, than growing on an allotment, or in traditional garden beds and borders.

Small-scale gardening also gives us a uniquely intimate relationship with our plants. When immediately outside our doors and windows, we are far more likely to give them just a few minutes of our undivided attention every day, rather than neglecting them and then struggling to dedicate hours at the weekend catching up.

Plants kept close at hand are easy to monitor, which means you are more likely to spot any problems early. You will notice, for example, if plants are struggling from a lack of water, and give them a drink before it's too late, or spot weeds when they are still at the seedling stage, and nip them out — this stops them from flowering and scattering seed, which would cause much bigger problems in a few weeks' time!

AMAZING GROWING OPPORTUNITIES

Making the most of every inch of space, squeezing growing spots out of unusual and unique places, can often result in the establishment of individual microclimates. Balconies and windowsills, for example, are often positioned between other flats and houses, so they can have an aspect and temperature that are quite different from those of the broader climate around them.

Your small area may be shady or overlooked, but if it is high up and hemmed in by buildings and walls, it is also likely to be sheltered and have slightly higher temperatures than the surrounding area, which could provide amazing growing opportunities.

Just a few extra degrees could be all you need to grow more tender and unusual plants than in a conventional garden. Sheltered sites are far less likely to suffer from frost, which could lead to enjoying home-grown figs or tending a tropical-style oasis right outside your back door.

Your plants can also flower earlier and for longer. Dahlias and other such plants that usually get knocked back by the first frosts may well be flowering long into winter. You may also get crops such as strawberries earlier than in a conventional garden, and lettuces all year round.

LESS HARDY PLANTS FOR A TROPICAL TOUCH

Bottlebrush (*Callistemon citrinus* 'Splendens')
Banana (*Musa basjoo*)
Canna (*Canna indica*)
Begonia (*Begonia*)
Soft tree fern (*Dicksonia antarctica*)
Japanese sago palm (*Cycas revoluta*)
Canary Island date palm (*Phoenix canariensis*)
Chusan palm (*Trachycarpus fortunei*)
Citrus, such as lemon and kumquat
(*Citrus* x *meyeri* 'Meyer', *Citrus japonica*)
Olive (*Olea europaea*)

CANNA

NURTURE YOUR CREATIVITY

If a garden space isn't obviously available, it forces us to be creative. Consider everywhere as a potential growing spot and take inspiration from the resources you have. Gardening doesn't have to be limited to the horizontal plane. Exploit the walls around you by putting up shelves and hanging planters, and turn railings and banisters into supports for climbers to scramble up and over. The opportunities are there – it's just up to you to find them.

BRINGING THE OUTSIDE IN

One of the best things about growing plants on a balcony, doorstep or windowsill is their proximity to home. Immediately visible from inside, even from the comfort of your armchair, these little gardens are so close by that they can resemble a beautiful house extension. Having greenery and nature in such close proximity creates an instant connection to the outside world. This creates a more soothing place, and can also make the property feel and look bigger.

Even the tiniest area, when filled with plants, can become a focal point, enhancing the look and feel of your home. You could even extend this effect by choosing your interior-design theme to complement your plants, picking out the same colours so that your room really does appear to extend beyond the boundaries of your four walls.

THE BENEFITS TO US

It's definitely possible to grow in any small space, and clearly it has its advantages, but is it worth the hassle? What differences can it make to our lives?

One of the main reasons people start growing is simply to have beautiful plants around them. The sheer vitality of plants can add another dimension to our lives, from the first crocus popping up in a window box to a bright summer hanging basket or the frosted leaves of a clipped box ball – and it's all happening just outside the window.

When growing a plant on a windowsill or balcony, all you have to do is reach out a hand to feel the soft, velvety leaves, sit quietly to notice its scent or hear the wind rustling through its branches.

WELL-BEING

The early humans were hunter-gatherers, living and eating according to the seasons, and today we retain some of their innate connection with plants. Growing and tending to plants helps us to stay connected with the changing seasons and the natural world, which enhances our well-being and our mental state.

Horticultural therapists have known for a long time that plants and gardening have lots of positive health benefits. Simply looking at plants makes us feel better, and the physical act of gardening is positively good for us. Watering pots, nipping out weeds and harvesting crops are a gentle distraction from our busy lives. Such tasks are also proven to increase brain activity and lower blood pressure. Every time we stretch and bend while gardening, we raise our heart rate and give our muscles and joints a work out. Growing plants keeps people fit and well in both mind and body!

SCENT

The heady scent of jasmine or the sweet fragrance of a rose is better than any synthetic perfume or air freshener, and when they are growing so close to your living space, the smell can be even more prevalent and enjoyable. Scented plants turn a space into a fragrant oasis. A powerfully scented plant, such as *Phlox paniculata*, tobacco plants (*Nicotiana sylvestris*) or *Rosa* 'Cornelia', will fill the air, seducing your senses every time you open the window or step outside. See pages 92–95 for more on scented plants for a small-space garden.

PHLOX

GROWING YOUR OWN

Growing your own food is a great way to start gardening, and, as an added bonus, there is fresh produce to eat at the end of the day. There are plenty of easy-to-grow fruits and vegetables that will thrive in tiny spaces. Annuals, such as radishes, can be grown from seed and are quick to crop, giving you a tasty harvest in just a few weeks, but a slower-growing perennial, such as a cordon apple or pear tree (a fruit tree trained to grow as a single stem), will be just as rewarding. Home-grown food comes with the added benefit of being fresh and healthy, and the reassurance of knowing exactly what is in it.

PRIVACY

Living in a crowded city, especially in an apartment block, generally means you have less privacy. Windows are often overlooked by neighbours or passers-by. Balconies, by their very nature, have no privacy at all. It can be difficult to relax out there, by yourself or with friends, and can make you not want to use your balcony at all. Plants can help to change all this.

Growing plants in window boxes, on steps and on balconies is a simple and cheap way to add a sense of privacy. Denser growing plants, such as sweet box (*Sarcococca confusa*), can create a screen, while plants with more delicate foliage, such as grasses (*Deschampsia cespitosa*) or Argentinian vervain (*Verbena bonariensis*) will add privacy without blocking out light or your view. Some trees and shrubs can lose their leaves in the autumn, so, if you use your space all year round, opt for evergreens.

POLLUTION PREVENTION

Urban living can be a noisy, dirty, brutal existence with cloying, belching traffic fumes all around and the rumble of planes up above. Amazingly, plants can help combat this and make our immediate environment healthier. Many plants are tolerant of urban pollution, thriving in even the most extreme situations, but they also absorb and filter fumes, preventing them from affecting us. All plants absorb carbon dioxide and turn it into oxygen, but the stems, leaves and branches can also trap particles in the air and absorb gaseous pollutants. These are then washed away when it rains, allowing us to breathe air that is less toxic.

Plants cut down on noise pollution, too. Planted around the perimeter of a balcony or around the front doorstep, they will help to reduce traffic noise. Plants grown on the walls of a building will further absorb irritating sounds.

THE BENEFITS TO WILDLIFE

All wildlife needs food, shelter and somewhere to breed, and the simple act of growing plants can provide just the right environment for this. As wildlife habitats in the countryside are reduced or disappear completely, green spaces in towns and cities are more important than ever.

Even the tiniest space or pot can make a difference to local wildlife – a window box planted with flowering plants can provide bees, butterflies and other pollinators, such as lacewings and hoverflies, with valuable nectar – it will also give you a brilliant view of them all coming and going. Each one of your tiny habitats will create green places where wildlife can rest and feed, which will have a positive impact on the gardens of your fellow growers in the neighbourhood. If you're growing on a high-up ledge or balcony, just remember to ensure there is sufficient shelter from the wind to help flying insects reach your plants.

YOU MIGHT SEE

BEES, such as honeybees and bumblebees, may visit your plants. Solitary bees might nest harmlessly in the mortar of your walls. They will be buzzing around your plants from as early as February right up until the first frosts.

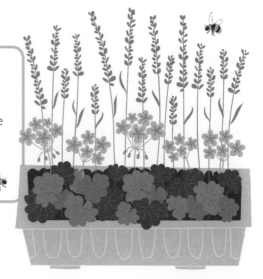

BUTTERFLIES AND MOTHS gather nectar from a variety of plants, particularly those with nectar-rich, scented flowers, such as honeysuckle (*Lonicera periclymenum*). Many species are in decline, but you should be able to see the red admiral, peacock and painted lady butterflies, and the elephant hawk moth feeding at dusk.

HOVERFLIES, despite their resemblance to bees or wasps, are true flies and definitely won't sting you! They drink nectar and eat pollen and aphids, and can be seen from early spring through to late autumn.

LACEWINGS are pretty, green insects with clear membranous wings. They are invaluable for feeding on sap-sucking aphids. They are seen from late spring to late summer, more often at night than during the day.

LADYBIRDS are fondly known as the gardener's friend. These bright beetles live off aphids and other small insects, and are easy to spot due to their flash of bright red. Look out through the winter for clusters of them hibernating in the sheltered corners of your balcony or ledge.

THE BENEFITS TO THE ENVIRONMENT

Plants and tiny gardens in towns and cities can have a vital beneficial effect on the wider community and environment around them.

COMMUNITY AND CRIME

A planted balcony or windowsill is a joy to see, but you may find it's not just your own life that is enhanced. Turning even the smallest space into a beautiful oasis can be such a welcoming sight that it may inspire your neighbours to also give it a go, transforming your neighbourhood into a colourful and vibrant place to live.

Remarkably, this can help cut down on crime, too. A green neighbourhood is more likely to have a sense of community pride, not just for those who helped to create it but for everyone else who lives there. Litter, graffiti and crime are less evident in greener neighbourhoods. In addition, plants themselves can physically discourage criminals: a shrewd choice of prickly or spiky plants around windows and balconies will make thieves think twice.

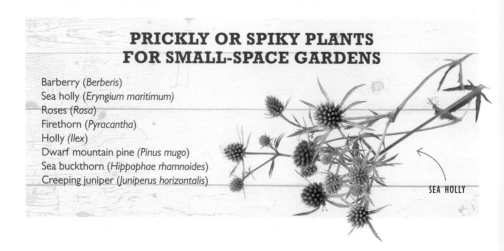

PRICKLY OR SPIKY PLANTS FOR SMALL-SPACE GARDENS

Barberry (*Berberis*)
Sea holly (*Eryngium maritimum*)
Roses (*Rosa*)
Firethorn (*Pyracantha*)
Holly (*Ilex*)
Dwarf mountain pine (*Pinus mugo*)
Sea buckthorn (*Hippophae rhamnoides*)
Creeping juniper (*Juniperus horizontalis*)

SEA HOLLY

URBAN TEMPERATURE REGULATORS

Even the smallest green space can help reduce urban temperatures, insulate buildings and prevent flooding. Built-up areas are naturally warmer than the surrounding countryside. Roads and walls absorb and trap the heat that radiates from buildings and cars – a town can have an ambient temperature three degrees warmer than the countryside.

Growing trees and plants can help to reduce these high temperatures in the following ways:

- Trees cast shade, creating cooler areas.
- Plants naturally lose water through their leaves, which helps to bring down temperatures.
- Planting around buildings, on walls, roofs and balconies, helps to insulate these spaces, reducing the absorption of heat in the summer and loss of it in winter.

Streets with plants and trees are significantly cooler in summer than those without, which is healthier for us, cuts down on our heating and air conditioning bills and reduces energy use.

FLOOD CONTROL

Plants also help to control water run-off and prevent flooding. The soil and compost that plants are grown in soak up rainwater. This can stop it flowing straight off a balcony, onto the streets below and into the already-overloaded drainage system, which, in times of heavy rain, can lead to water build-up and, eventually, flooding. If you have the space, catching rainwater in a water butt connected to a downpipe, or even just an open tank, will help even more. You can then use this water on drier days to give your plants a good drink.

SMALL SPACE CHALLENGES

Growing in small spaces presents its own set of unique challenges and, to be a successful small-space gardener, it's crucial to know what these are before you start.

LACK OF SPACE

The most obvious challenge of gardening in a small space is, clearly, the restriction on space: the smaller the space, the less flexible it is. Having just a tiny ledge, a single front step or narrow strip of balcony can be frustrating, but it's not impossible to grow here. The very smallest of places can actually inspire us to make creative use of every inch of what we have.

Windowsills, steps and ledges can support troughs and containers; a balcony floor can house a container pond and small raised bed; baskets can be hung from the eaves; and planters can be fixed to the walls. Even the railing around the edge of a balcony can be used to support climbers or hang pocket planters.

LACK OF SOIL

It's unlikely there will be any soil in your space, so a combination of containers – of any size, material and design you choose – are going to form your garden (see page 111 for everything you need to know about this).

FINDING THE RIGHT BALANCE

A small-space garden is a great way to create your own private oasis in a big city. It can be tricky, however, when using plants to create privacy (see page 18), to do so without making your space feel dark, enclosed and out of context with its environment. Rather than dense planting around and in every space, take the time to work out the areas that are most exposed and focus on growing there – the trick is to balance the feeling of privacy while still letting in light and enjoying the view. You could try the following:

- Use a semi-transparent screening made from rush or woven willow and hazel (available from most garden centres).
- Grow a living fence with climbing plants, such as clematis, scrambling up trellis, over railings or hanging from planters above windows.
- Plant hedging, if you have the space, using a mix of light plants, such as grasses, and shrubs, rather than dense plants.
- For privacy from overhead, use trees, a hanging basket obscuring the line of sight or, if there's room, plants trained up a pergola.

BALCONY-SPECIFIC CHALLENGES

WEIGHT Balconies are usually purpose-built, and although they are designed to support a number of people (so a few extra pots shouldn't be a problem), there will be weight restrictions to what you can grow there. If you have ambitious plans, check the weight-bearing load in your property deeds or consult a surveyor or structural engineer before you invest in plants and containers.

PERMISSION Depending on what you want to create on your balcony, you may need to seek the relevant planning permission. If you're planning on growing somewhere that's not officially a balcony, such as an area of roof space or a fire escape, you may first need planning or landlord permission.

DRAINAGE Balconies and roofs are generally built with a slight gradient so that rainwater flows away easily into drains and gullies. Check the gradient on your growing space and place pots so that they don't block the flow of rain run-off.

SAFETY It's vital your space has a secure barrier around it, so check any railings or bannisters are fixed firmly before you start growing on them. They must be strong enough to support plants or trellis and screening. Secure pots and planters with brackets or wires to stop them blowing or toppling over the edge to the ground below, and check they can't be used as steps for children to climb onto.

WINDOWSILL-SPECIFIC CHALLENGES

A windowsill may be all the available space you have or could provide an additional piece of much-needed space. However tiny it is, there is no reason why it can't be used to create your own miniature garden. Just consider the following issues before you start:

WEIGHT Check the strength of your sill before buying pots.

SIZE Measure your sill carefully and get the biggest, widest and deepest container it can support.

SAFETY Heavy pots are more stable than lighter ones. Always secure boxes onto the sill with brackets or wires stretched across the front to stop them falling off in the wind.

LEVELS Make sure your box is level on the ledge or it will slip down. Add wedges underneath the front, if you need to.

DIFFICULT GROWING CONDITIONS

CROTON

When you're growing in small, and possibly unusual, places, particularly up high, you will be forced to garden in conditions that are far from ideal. In a traditional garden, you have the flexibility and freedom to choose where your plants go to give them the best possible chance, but in a small space you just have to go with what you've got. Details on dealing with the most common tricky growing conditions are covered on the following pages.

SHADE

When you're squeezing growing space into the smallest places, it's inevitable that shade is going to be a problem. Buildings, walls and trees all cast shade. Balconies are almost always shaded by another balcony above, and if your growing space faces north or east, it's likely to be shrouded in shade for most, if not all, of the day.

Although plants need sunlight to survive, the amount of shade they can cope with varies. Each plant has its own needs so, before you start, you need to know what the light levels are in your spot. Get to know your space and work out where and when shade is cast. Watch how the sun moves across it, noting where the main areas of sun and shade are throughout the day, and how this changes with the seasons. Extremes of both can pose their own set of issues and will dictate which plants you can and can't grow.

SUMMER

SPRING/AUTUMN

WINTER

DIFFERENT TYPES OF SHADE

The degrees of shade vary, and there is more than one type – the trick is to know the different depths and types of shade that are cast across your own growing space.

DENSE SHADE Shade caused by buildings that block out light completely.

DAPPLED SHADE Blotchy shade is cast by overhanging trees.

LIGHT SHADE Spaces that receive sun for just a couple of hours a day but are generally screened from direct sunlight by an obstacle, such as a high wall or group of trees.

PARTIAL SHADE Areas open to the sky that may receive two to six hours of full sun at midsummer, but trees or buildings block out direct sunlight as the sun moves across the sky.

FULL SUN Open to direct sunlight for most of the day and not shaded by buildings or trees.

REMEMBER

Plenty of plants that prefer a sunny spot will still grow perfectly happily in shade – they will just flower and fruit a little less.

WIND

Wind is one of the biggest challenges for high-up growing spaces. Exposed to the harshest of elements, plant stems snap, leaves are buffeted and shredded, reducing their ability to take up water, and growth is stunted and slowed. High winds dry out compost and leaves, and young plants can be knocked back completely, even killed. If you live near the coast, the salt carried on the wind can also have damaging effects.

POTS AWAY

Consider carefully the type of pot you use in a windy spot. The lighter the pot, the more likely it is to be scattered across your balcony or toppled over completely. Secure and anchor pots, particularly any containing tall trees and shrubs, the leaves of which will act like sails in high winds. Tie them to railings or weigh them down with a stone mulch, or choose shallow, heavy planters and terracotta pots, which are far more stable than plastic ones.

BRACE YOURSELF

The simplest solution is to create a simple windbreak to protect your plants (and yourself) against the wind. This will block your view a little but the compromise is worth it for the transformative results – the shelter will increase the range of plants you'll be able to grow, and your balcony will be a warmer and more comfortable place to be. It will also enable pollinating insects to reach your flowers and reduce moisture loss in the soil.

Before you start, work out the direction the prevailing wind is coming from. This can change with the season, but you can check this information online.

Use the perimeter railings of a balcony as support to secure a semi-permeable barrier against the wind. An effective windbreak should only be 50 per cent solid – a solid wall would block the wind completely and cause a new problem when it forces the wind up and over it to land with even greater force right on top of your plants.

An artificial windbreak bought from a garden centre would provide instant shelter, but a planted screen made from a mix of shrubs and some small trees (see the box below for specific examples) is much nicer and longer lasting. It is also better at filtering the wind. Hedging with wind-tolerant plants is the greenest option, or look in your local garden centre for trellising and screens made from woven bamboo or rush, or hurdles made from willow or hazel.

PLANTS FOR A WINDBREAK

Black bamboo/ golden bamboo
(*Phyllostachys nigra, P. aurea*)
Four-stamen tamarisk (*Tamarix tetandra*)
Common lilac (*Syringa vulgaris*)
Dwarf mountain pine (*Pinus mugo*)
Daisy bush (*Olearia*)
Wilson's honeysuckle (*Lonicera nitida*)
Japanese pittosporum (*Pittosporum tobira*)

COMMON LILAC

DROUGHT AND SUN EXPOSURE

Balconies and ledges are often blasted by drying winds or exposed to the baking rays of the sun. Yours may be in a rain shadow cast by overhanging balconies or walls, or you may simply have no easy access to water. If you recognise any one of these problems, then your plants are in danger of becoming parched and drying out.

COMBATING DROUGHT

A lack of water is the main cause of plant death, and to avoid it you will need to keep a regular eye on your plants, checking them every day in hot summers. The easiest solution is to grow drought-tolerant plants, but you can also help by:

- Always giving plants the biggest pots you can.
- Making sure your plants have the very best growing medium by opting for a soil-based compost rather than a peat-based one, which dries out quicker.
- Mixing plenty of organic matter, such as homemade compost or animal manure, into the compost to improve the soil structure and increase its moisture-holding capacity.
- Adding water-retaining granules to the compost in pots where plants might struggle, such as hanging baskets.
- Always adding a layer of mulch, such as gravel, bark or pebbles, to the compost surface after planting to prevent moisture evaporating from the soil.
- Keeping on top of weeds to stop them competing with your plants for moisture in the compost.

INTENSE SUNSHINE AND LIGHT

Gardening up high can often mean a balcony exposed to endless glorious sunshine. Although this may seem a joy compared with the potential gloom of growing in a low spot shrouded in shade, too much sun exposure can lead to extreme temperatures and scorched, dry plants.

Lots of plants can cope happily in these conditions, but you may want to create shade to make conditions slightly less extreme for both you and your plants. You could try the following:

- Grow taller plants, strategically placed, to cast shade over your seating area or over less tolerant plants. Place pots of dense, bushy plants, such as bamboo (*Fargesia rufa*), or small trees, such as mountain pine (*Pinus mugo*), at the edges of your space.
- Protect plants with shade screens of rush or fabric attached to balcony railings.
- String up shade sails or canopies over and across the growing space.

Chapter 2

GETTING
IT RIGHT

The old gardening maxim 'right plant, right place' is never more true than when dealing with small spaces. The most successful gardeners will know their site well, spending plenty of time in it, perhaps with a notebook, observing its aspect and the presence of any sun, shade and wind exposure. Appreciating and understanding these challenges will help you choose the best plants for your plot. Compared with the relative flexibility of a larger garden, however, the microclimates formed in small spaces can make this quite a challenge!

The first pages of this chapter guide you in what to look for and other things to consider before greening your small space. Following this, the plant files in this chapter detail a range of wonderful plants that will thrive in small spaces, from deepest shade to intense sun spots. This chapter helps you to recognise certain adaptations (such as narrow, silvery leaves that minimise water loss) so that you'll be able to find the right plants for you and your small-space garden.

KNOWING YOUR SITE

Once you're aware of all the problems and challenges a small space might have, it's important to work out exactly the nature of your own site. Before you can do anything, you need to know certain things. For example, assessing how you access your growing space is crucial in order for you to know exactly what you can and can't grow. Also, before you start, you need to know where your water is going to come from.

ACCESS

It can be tricky to fit all the necessary items, such as pots, compost, tools and anything else you need, into your small space. Balconies, windowsills and other, more ingenious growing spots can usually only be reached by going through the house, and involve navigating narrow doorways and steep stairs. The route you have to take will dictate the size and types of plants you can grow and the materials you use. Lugging heavy pots, endless bags of compost and tall trees up to your flat may be difficult if you live high up and don't have a lift.

Before you get stuck in, make sure you do the following:
- Work out your route, checking the width of doorways, windows, stairwells and landings.
- See if it's possible to winch things directly onto your balcony from outside the building.
- If it's easier, ask neighbours if you can bring things through their flat.
- Protect your home by laying down plastic sheeting and taping cardboard over doorframes and windowsills.

WATER

When you're creating growing spaces in spots that aren't typical gardens or where access is not easy, there's rarely a convenient outdoor tap. In fact, your space may not be anywhere near a water source at all. This can make watering your plants difficult and, combined with the drying winds and intense heat so often found up high, your plants will soon be desperate for a drink.

If you've just got a few window boxes to tend, then filling up a watering can from the kitchen tap can be all you need, but anything more than that and the regular task of watering can become an endless slog through the flat with heavy cans of sloshing water.

Here are some tips for keeping your plants well watered and healthy:

- The best solution is to install an outdoor tap to fill your cans or connect a hose to.
- If you have the space, fit a rainwater butt to guttering or downpipes outside, or leave large shallow containers or tanks to collect rainwater as it falls. You can use these to fill watering cans, plus you'll save water.
- Make sure window boxes are placed so you can tend to and water them easily, preferably by simply leaning out of your window. If this is awkward, check you can water from the ground outside with a hose and long-handled lance.
- For hard-to-reach planters, look for pots with built-in reservoirs or install a drip-irrigation system.

CHOOSING THE RIGHT PLANTS

Once you've assessed your site and know exactly what conditions you have and where, you can work out the types of plants your garden can have. Choose the most suitable plant for each place, and your small-space garden will thrive.

Avoid picking plants just because you like them or because you saw them in full bloom in the garden centre. Simply choosing a plant in this way and then forcing it to grow in conditions it can't cope with will result in hard work and frustration for you and a weak, stressed, even dead, plant.

For example, it's essential you know how much light your growing space has so you can choose the right plants to grow there. Sunlight is essential for photosynthesis and therefore for all plants (except parasitic ones) to survive. Not enough light can lead to stunted growth and, eventually, death.

AMAZING ADAPTATIONS

As plants in the wild have evolved, they have developed an amazing variety of adaptations that help them not just survive, but thrive in many different and often stressful conditions and habitats. These adaptations make it possible for plants to cope with life in the dense shade of a forest, or the extreme bright light on a mountainside, or to live happily in an area with a lack of water or nutrients.

To survive in these situations, plants have, over thousands of years, evolved unique anatomical features or adopted a particular lifestyle. For example, the spikes of a cactus are actually modified leaves that reduce moisture loss and protect it against predators, while other plants, such as herbaceous perennials, become dormant when conditions get really tough in order to conserve energy.

Although these strategies can make a plant resilient, they are specialised and therefore make it difficult for that plant to survive anywhere else. This is why a particular plant will often only grow naturally in one kind of habitat. All the more reason why you should make sure you only choose plants that are happy with the conditions you have at home.

PLANTS FOR SHADE

Plants that can cope with shade are those that originate from forests and woodlands. They have evolved to thrive beneath dense tree canopies, where the soil is either damp and rich with the humus of decaying plant and animal matter, or thin and very dry due to the thick tree cover that only rarely allows rainfall to reach the ground.

Balconies and other urban small spaces are often steeped in shade, which can make many gardeners despair because they believe it is impossible to grow anything there or that they are doomed to grow boring plants with few or no flowers. They couldn't be more wrong! Shade adds depth to a garden, and the plants that can tolerate it are some of the most arresting and interesting on earth.

AVOIDING SHADE

In the deep shade of the forest floor, some plants deal with the low light levels by avoiding the shade completely, growing away from it and into the light. They focus their energy into producing long stems, rather than roots, and fewer leaves. For instance, some climbers can survive by growing up through the dark of the trees and out into the nourishing rays of the sun. Others, such as wood anemones (*Anemone nemorosa*) and bluebells (*Hyacinthoides non-scripta*), come into growth and flower early in the year, well before the trees in the forest are in leaf.

SHADE LOVERS

Plants that love living in the shade are called 'sciophilous'. To survive, they need a degree of shade that would likely stunt or even kill another plant.

WOOD ANEMONE

THRIVING IN SHADE

Other plants adapt to the low-light conditions to thrive in the shade. These are often efficient energy users. These plants have broader, wider leaves so that each leaf can catch as much sunlight as possible, but they are also very thin so they don't require too much energy to produce. Such plants include Japanese aralia (*Fatsia japonica*), hosta (*Hosta*), coral bells (*Heuchera*), heart-leaf bergenia (*Bergenia cordifolia*) and Japanese farfugium (*Farfugium japonicum*).

These plants can have increased amounts of chlorophyll in their leaves to maximise sunlight absorption, which makes their foliage very dark, glossy and green. Examples include bear's breech (*Acanthus mollis*), sweet box (*Sarcococca confusa*), leopard plant (*Ligularia dentata*) and Portugal laurel (*Prunus lusitanica*).

HOSTA FORTUNEI

BOX-LEAVED HONEYSUCKLE

Many plants, such as Japanese spurge (*Pachysandra terminalis*), box-leaf azara (*Azara microphylla*) and box-leaved honeysuckle (*Lonicera pileata*), have small, inconspicuous flowers and fruit to conserve energy.

Some have camouflaging strategies such as mottled leaves to stop animals eating them. Look for Japanese laurel (*Aucuba japonica*), lungwort (*Pulmonaria*) and Siberian bugloss (*Brunnera macrophylla*).

HEUCHERA 'PARIS'

PLANT FILE
SHADE

HONEYSUCKLE

There are shade plants to suit every situation, from shrubs to climbers and hanging baskets. Many have stunning textures, leaf colours and flowers. Use foliage plants, with their beautiful glossy greens and textures, as a backdrop and then lift your display with variegated leaves, such as *Carex oshimensis* 'Evergold'. Use plants with white or pastel flowers, such as Japanese anemone (*Anemone hupehensis* var. *japonica*), which will help to lift and brighten even the darkest spot. Many shade-loving plants also like moist soil, so add plenty of organic matter, such as home-made compost, when planting. Add mulch after planting and make sure plants are watered regularly.

EDIBLES FOR SHADE

Most fruiting crops need sun to flower, fruit and ripen, so avoid growing these in a shady spot. However, leafier crops, such as salads, chard and spinach, should grow quite happily and are far less likely to bolt when grown in shade. Roots, such as beetroot and radish, won't mind the cooler conditions. Runner bean, French bean and garden peas will grow successfully, as will the shade-loving herbs parsley, chervil, chives, coriander and mint. Acid cherry and plum 'Victoria' are also both shade-tolerant and happy grown against a north-facing wall.

CLIMBERS FOR WALLS OR RAILINGS
CHOCOLATE VINE
(*Akebia quinata*)
Bright-green, three-lobed leaves. Scented maroon-purple flowers in spring.

CLEMATIS
(*Clematis* spp.)
Look for Austrian clematis (*C. alpina*), with its nodding purple flowers in spring, or purple clematis (*C. viticella*) cultivars, which flower in midsummer. Need support to climb.

CLIMBING HYDRANGEA
(*Hydrangea anomala* ssp. *petiolaris*)
Pretty heart-shaped leaves and bronze, woody stems. A froth of white flowers in summer.

HONEYSUCKLE
(*Lonicera*)
Deciduous climbers with heavily scented flowers in summer and autumn, which are sometimes followed by red or black fruit. Loved by pollinators. Look for *Lonicera periclymenum* 'Graham Thomas' or late Dutch honeysuckle (*L. periclymenum* 'Serotina'). Need support to climb.

Climbing hydrangea will support itself against a wall.

GROUND COVER AND LOW GROWERS

BIG BLUE LILYTURF
(Liriope muscari)
Blade-like leaves all year round with wands of purple flowers in autumn.

CREEPING DOGWOOD
(Cornus canadensis)
Creamy white bracts nestle among green leaves in spring. Scarlet berries follow in autumn.

LADY'S MANTLE
(Alchemilla mollis)
Scalloped bright-green leaves with a foam of acid-yellow flowers in summer. Leaves catch water droplets after a rain shower.

CONTAINERS AND HANGING BASKETS

ORANGE NEW ZEALAND SEDGE
(Carex testacea)
Small evergreen grasses with a mounding hummocky habit. Cope well with shade, although *C. testacea* can lose some of its brightness.

MAINDENHAIR FERN, SPLEENWORT FERN, POLYPODY
(Adiantum, Asplenium and *Polypodium)*
Thrive in all shade. Look for those that suit your particular dry or damp spot.

CORAL BELLS
(Heuchera)
Compact evergreen plants that come in an amazing range of ruffled leaf colours, from lime-green to black to toffee and scarlet red. They also have spikes of delicate flowers in the summer.

HELLEBORE
(Helleborus)
Nodding cup-shaped flowers and leathery deep green leaves. Flowers late winter to spring.

CRANESBILL
(Geranium)
Spreading leafy perennials. Come in a wide range of colours, invaluable for creating a flash of colour in a shady spot.

SIBERIAN BUGLOSS 'JACK FROST'
(Brunnera macrophylla 'Jack Frost')
Heart-shaped leaves dusted with silver. Bright forget-me-not flowers in spring.

HELLEBORE

EVERGREENS AND SHRUBS FOR SCREENING AND PRIVACY

JAPANESE SPURGE
(Pachysandra terminalis)
Forms dense mats of shiny serrated leaves. Clusters of tiny white flowers in summer.

SWEET BOX
(Sarcococca ssp.*)*
A dense evergreen shrub with deep glossy leaves. Produces sweetly scented winter flowers that are followed by shiny black berries.

LESSER PERIWINKLE
(Vinca minor)
A fast-growing creeper. Lavender-blue flowers through spring and summer.

RAKAI HEBE
(Hebe rakaiensis)
Rounded shrubby evergreen with neat leaves and summer flowers.

Lady's mantle fares well in shade and also makes a good cut flower.

PLANTS FOR HIGH LIGHT LEVELS

A south- or west-facing space, such as a balcony, will be drenched in full sun for most of the day. Other growing spots, such as a roof or tiny open terrace, may also be at risk of overexposure to the sun's scorching rays and intense light. Too much sunlight can cause scorched leaves, wilting, poor growth and even death, so plants need to find ways to protect themselves.

STONECROP

HEAT AND LIGHT PROTECTION

Plants that originate in areas with high light levels, such as high on a mountaintop or in the desert, have developed a variety of clever leaf modifications to help them survive. Intense light and sunshine invariably causes moisture loss in the leaves and soil, so plants that have adapted to tolerate high light levels generally also have an increased tolerance to heat and drought (see pages 52–57).

Plants that have adapted to high light levels have thick leaves, often with a waxy layer, to protect them against the heat of the sun. The waxy coating helps to reflect the heat of the sun. Examples include bearded irises (*Iris germanica*), cabbage palm (*Cordyline australis*) and stonecrop (*Sedum*).

BEARDED IRIS

Light- and heat-tolerant plants, such as rosemary (*Rosmarinus*), can have small, narrow needle-like leaves, which means there is less surface area to absorb light and therefore less water lost from the leaves. Others such as rock rose (*Cistus*), often have shorter stems and branches for the same reason.

ROSEMARY

To avoid high light levels, a plant's leaves can be coated in tiny hairs, which create shade. These hairs also trap moisture by slowing the movement of air across the leaf. Examples of these plants are lamb's ear (*Stachys byzantina*), geranium (*Pelargonium*) and Russian sage (*Perovskia atriplicifolia*).

GERANIUM

SUMMER LEAVES

In the scorching conditions of the Mediterranean, some plants produce special 'summer leaves' to help them cope with the harsh sun. For example, while the winter leaves of sage (*Salvia*) have shrivelled and died, the small summer leaves with curled edges protect the plant against the intense light and heat.

PLANT FILE
HIGH LIGHT LEVELS

Plants that enjoy full sun are some of the most jubilant and exotic-looking you will find. Keep in mind, also, that creating some shade will cut down on your watering time, and add a bit of depth and variety to your small-space garden.

EDIBLES FOR LIGHT

Many crops will grow well in high light levels, but you will also be able to grow crops that can't cope with other extreme conditions. For example, fruiting crops such as chillies, peppers and tomatoes will thrive if you start them early in the season, but so will grapes, citrus, figs, olives and melons. Sun-loving herbs, such as basil, sage, rosemary, thyme and chives, should also do well.

CONTAINER AND HANGING-BASKET PLANTS

GERANIUM
(Pelargonium)
Classic Mediterranean flowering plant with pretty, sometimes scented, leaves. Look for trailing types to spill over the edges of containers.

YARROW
(Achillea spp.*)*
Ferny, feathery foliage supports flat flower heads that bees love.

BEARDED IRIS
(Iris germanica)
Stately plants with ruffle-petalled flowers in a range of bright and exotic colours.

SAGE
(Salvia)
Hooded flowers grow in a range of rich shades and pastel hues during summer.

SHRUB VERBENA
(Lantana camara)
Tropical looking with orange flowers that change colour as they age.

COSMOS
(Cosmos)
Bright daisy-like flowers over fine lacy leaves bloom from early summer through to the autumn.

GROUND COVER AND LOW GROWERS

AUBRIETA 'PURPLE CASCADE'
(Aubrieta 'Purple Cascade')
Produces a mass of bright-purple flowers in spring and will spread through raised beds and tumble over containers.

Bearded iris has stunning flowers that come in a range of colours.

Armand clematis is a twining, evergreen climber for high, light spaces.

TRAILING BELLFLOWER
(Campanula poscharskyana)
An easy-to-grow scrambler with
star-shaped blue flowers.

LAMB'S EAR
(Stachys byzantina)
Aptly named, with soft, grey felted leaves
that form a dense carpet of silver.
Produces spikes of pretty pink flowers
throughout summer.

AFRICAN DAISY
(Osteospermum)
Produces carpets of large daisy
flowers in summer over spreading
mounds of foliage.

CLIMBERS FOR WALLS OR RAILINGS

ASIATIC JASMINE
(Trachelospermum asiaticum)
A self-clinging, evergreen climber with
creamy-white flowers that will clothe a
wall or railings in just a few seasons.

ARMAND CLEMATIS
(Clematis armandii)
Twining evergreen climber that
produces snow-white fragrant flowers
in spring. Ribbed, leathery leaves are
bronze when young.

POTATO TREE 'GLASNEVIN'
(Solanum crispum 'Glasnevin'*)*
A spectacular climber with clusters of
purple flowers. Needs shelter but can
be evergreen in mild winters.

EVERGREENS AND SHRUBS FOR SCREENING AND PRIVACY

COTTON LAVENDER
(Santolina chamaecyparissus)
Compact with aromatic grey foliage.
Yellow button-shaped flowers appear
in mid-to-late summer.

CRIMSON BOTTLEBRUSH 'SPLENDENS'
(Callistemon citrinus 'Splendens'*)*
Dazzling, fuzzy red flowers with interesting
seed heads. The narrow leaves are lemon
scented when crushed. Half hardy, but
should do well in a sheltered nook.

BASTARD SENNA 'CITRINA'
(Coronilla valentina spp. *glauca* 'Citrina'*)*
A low-growing, grey-leaved shrub that
produces clusters of lemon-yellow flowers
continuously from November to May.

ROCK ROSE
(Cistus spp.*)*
Produces masses of crumpled,
papery flowers throughout summer,
each lasting only a day.

SILVERBUSH
(Convolvulus cneorum)
Aptly named, with elegant silver leaves
and stems. White trumpet flowers last
until the first frosts.

ROCK ROSE

PLANTS FOR DRY CONDITIONS

Water is essential for all plants to survive. Without it, plants wilt, weaken and, eventually, die. The plants that can cope with life without regular water hail from the deserts and dry landscapes of the world. These areas have very scarce rainfall – often falling only two or three times a year – and the soil is rocky or sandy. The plants that live there have to be able to cope with both the lack of available water and the rapid evaporation of water that's in the soil and their leaves.

DRY AND BRIGHT

Plants that have adapted to tolerate drought generally also have an increased tolerance to high light levels (see pages 48–51).

DROUGHT TOLERANCE

Drought can be an issue in almost every small-space garden, whether it is exposed to full sun, pounded by the wind, hidden within a rain shadow or simply nowhere near a tap. Drought-tolerant plants, with their clever leaf adaptations, are the plants to grow.

Drought-tolerant plants, or xerophytes, have adapted to harsh, arid conditions by changing or modifying their physical appearance. They often grow slowly to reduce the amount of energy they expend and water they need, or they can have long roots that spread far into the ground searching for water. The most significant features of these plants, however, are the various leaf characteristics, developed to help them cope without water.

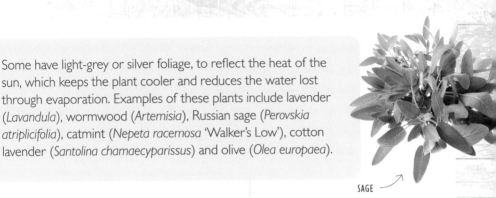

Some have light-grey or silver foliage, to reflect the heat of the sun, which keeps the plant cooler and reduces the water lost through evaporation. Examples of these plants include lavender (*Lavandula*), wormwood (*Artemisia*), Russian sage (*Perovskia atriplicifolia*), catmint (*Nepeta racemosa* 'Walker's Low'), cotton lavender (*Santolina chamaecyparissus*) and olive (*Olea europaea*).

SAGE

JUNIPER

A smaller leaf surface holds less heat and loses less moisture than bigger leaves, making them able to cope for longer with little or no water, so many desert plants, such as rosemary, pine (*Pinus*), juniper (*Juniperus*), wattle (*Acacia*) and thyme, have developed tiny needle-like leaves.

Succulent plants store water in their fleshy stems, leaves or tuberous roots. They can absorb large amounts of water over a short period of time, and their shallow but extensive root systems suck up water when it rains, sending it to the fleshy parts of the plant, which then swell up. Water gets stored for when there is no more water in the ground. Examples of these plants include stonecrop (*Sedum*), houseleek (*Sempervivum*), aloe (*Aloe*), agave (*Agave*), purslane (*Portulaca*), and aeonium (*Aeonium*).

PURSLANE

Fragrant oils, covering the surface of the leaves in a film, prevent evaporation and reduce moisture loss. Plants with fragrant leaves include thyme, geranium, curry plant (*Helichrysum italicum*), sage and rosemary.

PLANT FILE
DRY CONDITIONS

Many drought-tolerant plants are grown in gardens for their attractive silvery foliage or elegant succulent leaves, but lots of them also produce gorgeous flowers, and many have interesting forms and shapes. There are drought-tolerant plants (from trees and shrubs to annual seasonal bedding) for just about any spot, but for balcony and windowsill growing, look for compact, slow-growing plants (unless you want green cover quickly), with a long season of interest.

EDIBLES FOR DROUGHT

If drought or lack of water is an issue on your balcony, it's best to avoid growing thirsty crops like tomatoes, potatoes, cucumbers, courgettes or strawberries. However, leafy crops and herbs like chard, spinach, kale, fennel, thyme, lemon verbena and sage are all relatively drought-tolerant, as are garlic and onions. Goji berries and cape gooseberries are also worth growing.

CONTAINERS AND HANGING BASKETS
VERBENA
(Verbena bonariensis 'Lollipop' and V. rigida)
Stunning feature plants with clusters of purple flowers at the tips of slender stems in the summer and into autumn. Bees and butterflies love them.

LESSER QUAKING GRASS
(Briza minor)
Gorgeous tufted evergreen grass with delightful hanging purple and green flowers that turn to gold and shake in the breeze.

ICE PLANT
(Sedum spectabile)
Statuesque plants with fleshy, succulent leaves and large, flat heads of starry flowers late in the season. They are happy on very little soil and look lovely creeping across guttering, old sinks and low troughs.

MEXICAN FEATHER GRASS
(Stipa tenuissima)
An architectural grass with fluffy tufts of silvery green flowers at the end of the summer.

GERANIUM
(Pelargonium)
Classic, bright, Mediterranean flowers and pretty, sometimes scented, leaves. Trailing types will spill nicely over container edges.

Verbena's
tall flower spikes
add colour
and privacy.

AFRICAN DAISY
(Osteospermum)
Produces carpets of large daisy flowers in summer over spreading mounds of foliage.

EVERGREENS AND SHRUBS FOR SCREENING AND PRIVACY
ENGLISH LAVENDER
(Lavandula angustifolia 'Hidcote', *L. angustifolia* 'Miss Muffet')
Easy shrubs with silvery grey leaves and spikes of fragrant flowers in summer.

WORMWOOD 'POWIS CASTLE'
(Artemisia 'Powis Castle')
Beautiful, silvery scented foliage that can be lacy or bold. Insignificant flowers in late summer.

CALIFORNIAN LILAC
(Ceanothus 'Blue Mound')
A dense, low-growing shrub that produces a mass of powder-blue flowers in late spring.

GROUND COVER AND LOW GROWERS
LAMB'S EAR
(Stachys byzantina)
Aptly named, with soft grey felted leaves that form a dense carpet of silver in even the driest soils. Has spikes of pretty pink flowers through summer.

COBWEB HOUSELEEK
(Sempervivum arachnoideum)
One of the easiest plants to grow, spreads quickly and comes in a range of different leaf colours and patterns, all displayed in distinctive fleshy rosettes. Also has pretty flowers in summer.

ELEPHANT'S EARS 'PURPUREA'
(Bergenia cordifolia 'Purpurea')
Provides tough ground cover with large, leathery, evergreen leaves. Produces spikes of flowers in early-to-mid spring.

CLIMBERS FOR WALLS AND RAILINGS
COMMON JASMINE
(Jasminum officinale)
Gloriously scented, deciduous climber. Produces clusters of white flowers in summer.

COMMON PASSION FLOWER
(Passiflora caerulea)
A vigorous climber with exotic summer flowers and glossy green leaves. Produces edible (but not very tasty) orange fruits in the autumn.

PASSION FLOWER

The intricate
forms of succulents
are ideal for close
observation.

PLANTS FOR WINDY CONDITIONS

The many exposed sites of the world, such as bleak mountainsides and coastal situations, are some of the harshest on earth. There are cold, icy winds in winter and dry, scorching gales in summer. Plants that grow naturally in these exposed places have to be tough and determined. Many have the typical adaptations of drought-tolerant plants, while others have adapted specifically to their windy homes.

BLOWING A GALE

Winds batter the landscape, making plants bend and sway dramatically. They can shred and scorch leaves, break and twist fragile stems and branches, and tug and uproot shallow-rooted plants. Winds also dry out the leaf surface, causing leaf scorch and making it difficult to take up moisture in the soil. This leads to struggling, stunted plants. It also lowers the air temperature around plants, reducing growth further.

In persistent wind, plants close the pores, or stomata, on their leaves to reduce water loss. However, closing these pores limits the plant's ability to breath, and can slow growth considerably. An exposed balcony or rooftop can be a tough place to garden, but it is by no means impossible, and a shrewd choice of plants is the way to succeed.

WINDPROOF

Plants can be dwarf or low growing to stop them getting battered by gales, or they can form mats and cling to the ground to reduce their exposure to the wind. Examples of these plants include alpines, such as thrift (*Armeria maritima*), lady's mantle (*Alchemilla mollis*), pinks (*Dianthus*) and creeping Jenny (*Lysimachia nummularia*).

Wind-resistant plants have tougher and thicker stems that can bend and flex in the wind without snapping. Examples include grasses such as eulalia (*Miscanthus sinensis*) and pampas grass (*Cortaderia selloanal*), four-stamen tamarisk (*Tamarix tetandra*) and broadleaf (*Griselinia littoralis*).

RED-HOT POKER

SEA HOLLY

Many plants have small, narrow leaves to reduce wind resistance, such as sea holly (*Eryngium maritimum*), heathers (*Erica* spp. and *Calluna* spp.), red-hot poker (*Kniphofia* spp.), variegated Japanese pittosporum (*Pittosprum tobira* 'Nanum') and lavender.

CABBAGE PALM

Others have leaves that are quite the opposite: large sail-like leaves that get ripped to shreds by the wind. These 'rip zones' allow the leaves to get torn and shredded, which reduces wind resistance and any further damage to the plant. Examples of these plants include cabbage palm (*Cordyline australis*) and New Zealand flax (*Phormium tenax*).

Some plants, such as grasses, are able to physically roll their leaves to protect against the drying wind and reduce the evaporation of water.

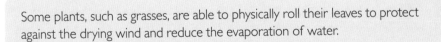

PLANT FILE
WINDY CONDITIONS

Although more fragile plants, such as leafy climbers, would last just days, there are many tenacious plants that will thrive in even the windiest spot. Reduce the wind's damaging effects with a barrier, and the growing opportunities are increased even further. In pots and raised beds, keep the compost level low so that the container sides offer extra protection, and mulch plants with a thick layer of gravel or shells to protect against the drying effects of the wind.

EDIBLES FOR WIND

Anything tall, such as sweetcorn, or climbing, will soon be torn to shreds in a windy spot. Choose low-growing crops, such as potatoes, salads, carrots, garlic and strawberries, and look for dwarf runner and French bean varieties. Blueberries, gooseberries and redcurrants should also cope well.

CLIMBERS
WINTER JASMINE
(*Jasminum nudiflorum*)
Cheery yellow flowers appear on bare, green stems in winter. A vigorous grower.

CLIMBING HYDRANGEA
(*Hydrangea anomala* spp. *petiolaris*)
A slow starter but will eventually romp across a wall. Heart-shaped leaves and a froth of lacy white flowers in early summer. Self-clinging.

EVERGREENS AND SHRUBS FOR SCREENING AND PRIVACY
SEA BUCKTHORN
(*Hippophae rhamnoides*)
A tall bushy maritime shrub with silvery leaves and attractive, edible orange berries.

BLACK ELDER
(*Sambucus nigra*)
Dramatic, lacy black leaves and pale-pink, scented flowers in late spring. Birds love the black autumn berries that follow.

LAVENDER
(*Lavandula* spp.)
Mounds of evergreen silver foliage and distinctively fragranced purple, pink or white flowers in summer.

ROSEMARY
(*Rosmarinus officinalis*)
Bushy evergreen with aromatic, edible leaves and spikes of purple or pink flowers. Look for the mat-forming variety.

Winter jasmine's yellow flowers brighten the dullest of winter days.

GRASSES
EULALIA
(Miscanthus sinensis)
Narrow silvery leaves and masses
of reddish-brown plumes that fade
to silver in the autumn.

MEXICAN/ROUGH FEATHER GRASS
(Stipa tenuissima/S. calamagrostis)
Compact grasses with thin, glaucous
leaves and fluffy or tufted golden plumes
that sway in the breeze.

BLUE FESCUE
(Festuca glauca)
A clump-forming compact grass
with bluish-green spiky flowers.

CONTAINERS AND HANGING BASKETS
ROSE CAMPION
(Lychnis coronaria)
Beautiful felted, silvery leaves and
stems, contrasting with vivid pink
flowers in late summer.

SMALL GLOBE THISTLE
(Echinops ritro)
Thistly globes of blue flowers are
loved by bees and butterflies.

WALLFLOWER 'BOWLES'S MAUVE'
(Erysimum 'Bowles's Mauve')
A very long bloomer, with bright
purple flowers and glaucous green
leaves and stems.

PERENNIAL PHLOX
(Phlox paniculata)
Trusses of lilac, pink red or white
flowers, deliciously scented, and a
favourite of butterflies and bees.

AFRICAN LILY
(Agapanthus africanus)
Blooms in late summer with globes
of trumpet-shaped blue flowers.

GROUND COVER AND LOW GROWERS
PINK
(Dianthus spp.)
Compact evergreens with
ruffled summer blooms, often
with a clove-like sent.

SEA THRIFT
(Armeria maritima)
Pretty grassy-green hummocks support
candy-pink flowers from late spring
through to the autumn.

BLACK MONDO
(Ophiopogon planiscapus 'Nigrescens')
Grass-like foliage that is almost black.
Small mauve flowers appear in summer,
followed by black berries.

PHLOX

Sea thrift is one of the hardiest plants for an exposed situation.

Chapter 3

SMALL-SPACE GARDENING PROJECTS

If you need inspiration, are after a particular look or have a challenging growing space, this chapter will suggest creative solutions for creating the small-space garden of your dreams.

These 12 simple projects show that you don't need acres of space to have a pond or lawn, and that it's even possible to grow something to eat in a small-space garden. Jungle-like foliage and sweetly scented flowers can be grown from mere pots and windowboxes, and you can do your bit to help ailing insect populations by planting a pollinator basket.

A LAWN IN A POT

Even the smallest of gardens can have a beautiful, lush green lawn! Grass is brilliantly simple to grow, requiring very little effort or attention, and will grow in any container, provided it has a minimum depth of about 15cm.

CHOOSING A CONTAINER

Wide, shallow planters, such as an old tin bath or wooden box, can become a contemporary feature. Alternatively, use a sturdy bucket or a large Tubtrug®. You could even use a raised bed, and it can double up as a seat. There are many simple DIY raised-bed kits on the market, made from wood, plastic or metal. Just choose the size and material that suit your space.

TURF OR SEED?

Turf is available to buy at garden centres and DIY shops, is very simple to lay and provides a lawn instantly. It is sold in metre-square strips and, although you should only need one or two pieces, it is more expensive than buying seeds.

Ideally, turf is laid in the autumn or spring; in the summer, it will need constant watering to stop it drying out. If you need more than a strip, stagger the joints, butting each piece of turf closely up against the next.

The directions on the following page demonstrate how to work with turf. You may wish to grow from seed, which will give you a greater choice of grass species – you may prefer a very fine grass in your feature pot, or need a shade-tolerant mix. Scatter seeds evenly across the compost at the rate recommended on the packet. It will take about a week to germinate and will need watering until it is established.

METHOD

Sprinkle a generous layer of sharp sand in the base of your container to help with drainage. This will also add weight and stability if you are intending to use your lawn container as a seat.

YOU WILL NEED:
- A container or raised bed
- Multipurpose compost
- Sharp sand
- Hand trowel
- Turf
- Sharp knife
- Watering can
- Shears or scissors

Fill to the brim with compost, firm it down well with your hands and then rake with a hand trowel until the surface is level.

Lay the turf over the compost and use a knife to trim the edges.

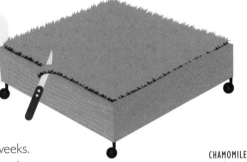

MAINTENANCE

Water well, particularly in the first few weeks. Keep your lawn pot neat and in shape by using shears or scissors to 'mow' it.

CHAMOMILE

ALTERNATIVES TO GRASS

Plant your pot with chamomile plants (*Chamaemelum*), which have scented leaves and flowers that are particularly pungent when touched or brushed against. Wildlife will love it too. Look for *Chamaemelum nobile* 'Treneague' which doesn't flower and keeps a more dense foliage than the flowering varieties.

A TUB OF SPUDS

Although potato plants take up a lot of room in the ground, they are actually an extremely simple and low-maintenance crop for containers. You may not get a huge harvest – just enough for a couple of meals – but it's well worth giving them a go. Rather than traditional main crop types, look for the more unusual new potatoes that are either unavailable or expensive to buy in the shops.

YOU WILL NEED:
- A large plastic tub, bag or pot at least 30cm deep
- Egg box or plastic tray for chitting
- Multipurpose compost
- Seed potatoes
- Potato fertiliser

METHOD

- Before planting, stand the seed potatoes in an old egg box or tray on a bright windowsill with the end bearing the most shoots (or eyes) facing upwards – a process known as chitting.
- When the shoots are 2–3cm long, they can be planted out. Two tubers are enough for a pot 30cm in diameter; three for a 40cm pot.
- If using a tub, make sure there are drainage holes in the bottom before you start planting.
- Fill the container with 20cm of potting compost and sprinkle in a little fertiliser.
- Plant the chitted potatoes shoot-end up and cover with another 10cm of compost. Water in.

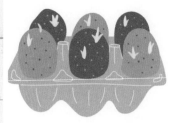

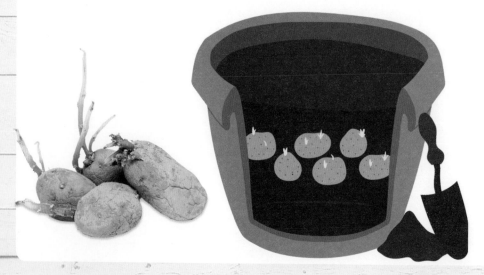

MAINTENANCE

Place your tub in a sunny spot and keep plants well watered. As the plants grow, keep covering their shoots and leaves with compost until you reach the top of the tub.

They should be ready to harvest when they are in flower.

WHAT TO PLANT

Look for first earlies, such as 'Winston', 'Riviera' and 'Accent' from January onwards. Second earlies, such as 'International Kidney', 'Charlotte' and 'Duke of York', should be available to buy from February. Depending on which potatoes you grow, plant them from mid-to-late spring. New potatoes are best eaten straight away, so only harvest your crop when you need them.

BEWARE BLIGHT

Blight is the biggest killer of potatoes, but grow only early varieties and you should avoid it – that way, your crop will be out of the tub and eaten before it strikes.

A JUNGLE OF CLIMBERS AND CREEPERS

Climbing plants are endlessly useful for clothing walls and fences. They are invaluable for providing privacy and shade on a balcony, and for their ability to transform a bare grey space into a vibrant green jungle. They also take up little space on the ground, leaving you with room for more plants or somewhere comfy to sit and enjoy the view.

YOU WILL NEED:
- A long low trough or pot the length of the area you wish to clothe (or a number of smaller troughs)
- Multipurpose compost
- Trowel
- Climbing plants
- Bamboo canes
- Garden twine
- Watering can

METHOD

Make sure your climbers have been watered well a few hours before planting.

Line your containers along the edge of the balcony and add compost until they are two-thirds full.

Before planting, plan out your arrangement. Combine an interesting balance of evergreen and deciduous and flowering plants in the container. Make sure that there is enough room between each plant for them to grow.

Take the climbers out of their pots and plant in. Make sure that the tops of their root balls are just below the rim of the container, then fill in around the root balls with compost to firm them in well.

Water the plants well and then guide your climbers on to the bamboo cane supports, tying them in with garden twine.

CLEMATIS

MAINTENANCE

Keep tying in the new stems until they are growing along their supports unaided.

Most evergreen climbers will need just a light prune to keep them in check, but deciduous plants are pruned according to when they flower – as a rule of thumb, those that flower before midsummer are pruned straight after flowering, while those that bloom from midsummer onwards are cut back in spring.

Clematis are arranged into pruning groups depending on when they flower (see page 131), so check which yours is before you prune.

WHAT TO PLANT

Climbers are too weak to support their own weight and instead use nearby plants, trees or walls to support them and help them grow up into the light. Some may need more help and support than others. Make sure you know what yours need and give them the appropriate trellis or wires before planting (see adaptations below).

CLIMBERS THAT SCRAMBLE

Climbers, such as climbing roses *(Rosa)*, have long flexible stems that are unable to climb on their own but have thorns that help them grab and grip onto supports. They will need guiding and tying in to supports, such as a trellis or wires.

CLIMBERS THAT CLING

Specialised 'adventitious' roots sprout from the stems of these plants and cling to whatever is nearby. This group of climbers, which includes ivy *(Hedera)* and climbing hydrangea *(Pileostegia viburnoides)*, needs no extra support.

CLIMBERS WITH TENDRILS

Tendrils are adapted from leaves or stems. They twine around supports and need a trellis or wires in order to climb. Examples of plants with tendrils are sweet peas *(Lathyrus odoratus)* and grape vines *(Vitis vinifera* 'Purpurea').

CLIMBERS THAT TWINE

These plants, which include clematis (*Clematis*), honeysuckle (*Lonicera*), nasturtium (*Tropaeolum*), beans and jasmine (*Jasminum),* have twining stems or leaves that twist around supports, such as wires or the stems of other plants.

CLIMBERS THAT STICK

These plants, such as Chinese Virginia creeper (*Parthenocissus henryana*), have stem tendrils with sticky sucker pads on the end that help them stick to their supports. They need no further help.

PLANT FILE
A JUNGLE OF CLIMBERS
AND CREEPERS

Whatever aspect or situation your small-space garden is in, there are climbers that will love it there. If your space is particularly exposed on one side, a long trough of climbers will conceal it perfectly. Choose a mix of evergreen and deciduous plants to ensure you have cover all year round. (Some of these plants include their pruning group – see page 131 for more information about pruning.)

EVERGREEN CLIMBERS FOR A SUNNY WALL
ASIATIC JASMINE
(Trachelospermum asiaticum)
Cream scented jasmine-like flowers and glossy green leaves, which are bronze when young in spring. Self-clinging.

POTATO TREE 'GLASNEVIN'
(Solanum crispum 'Glasnevin')
Purple flowers that have a bright-orange centre.

ARMAND CLEMATIS
(Clematis armandii)
Glossy leathery leaves and fragrant white flowers in spring. Pruning group 1.

COMMON PASSION FLOWER
(Passiflora caerulea)
Distinctive purple and cream flowers in summer followed by autumnal orange fruit.

EVERGREEN CLIMBERS FOR A SHADY WALL
COMMON IVY, PERSIAN IVY
(Hedera helix, H. colchica)
Glossy heart-shaped leaves in almost every shade of green and variegation. Great for wildlife.

CLIMBING HYDRANGEA
(Pileostegia viburnoides)
Slow growing but worth it for its showy mass of tiny white star-shaped flowers in late summer.

PURPLE CLEMATIS
(Clematis viticella)
Gorgeous deep-purple flowers in summer and autumn. Pruning group 3.

IVY

HOPS

DECIDUOUS CLIMBERS FOR A SUNNY WALL

SCOTTISH FLAME FLOWER
(Tropaeolum speciosum)
A scrambling plant with pretty leaves and scarlet flowers in summer.

KOLOMIKTA
(Actinidia kolomikta)
The heart-shaped leaves have splashes of pink and white at the tips. Fragrant white flowers appear in summer.

COMMON HOP
(Humulus lupulus 'Aureus')
Large, deeply lobed, acid-yellow leaves and golden cone-like flowers that dry out, persisting until the plant dies back in the autumn.

COMMON JASMINE
(Jasminum officinale)
Beautifully scented. Produces clusters of white flowers in summer.

DECIDUOUS CLIMBERS FOR A SHADY WALL

CHOCOLATE VINE
(Akebia quinata)
A pretty, twining climber with unusual maroon flowers that have a vanilla scent.

COMMON HONEYSUCKLE
(Lonicera periclymenum)
Bees and butterflies love the scented tubular flowers in summer. Fruit follows in autumn.

CLIMBING HYDRANGEA
(Hydrangea anomala spp. petiolaris)
Deep green, heart-shaped leaves and a froth of lacy white flowers in summer.

CHINESE VIRGINIA CREEPER
(Parthenocissus henryana)
Deeply divided, heavily veined green leaves turn to scarlet in autumn. Needs support until established.

JASMINE

A DROUGHT-HAPPY PLANTER

Your growing space may be in a rain shadow, up high or beaten by the wind, or you may just have little time for watering. A planter filled with a range of drought-tolerant plants will thrive whatever the weather throws at them.

YOU WILL NEED:
- Container or planter (minimum 30cm depth)
- Multipurpose compost
- Horticultural grit or perlite for improved drainage
- Drought-happy plants (choose from the list opposite)
- Pebbles for mulching

METHOD

Mix the compost and grit or perlite together at a ratio of 2:1 and fill your container two-thirds full.

Arrange your plants until you like the way they look and then plant, filling in with the compost mix as you go.

Firm down around the plants, water them in and then use more grit and pebbles to mulch and give an arid look.

PLANT FILE
A DROUGHT-HAPPY PLANTER

All these plants display the classic plant adaptations that help them cope with drought (see page 32). Many also grow on rocky mountainsides and cliff faces where there is little, poor soil. Use mat-forming and low-growing spurge and succulents at the front and edges and then fill in with lamb's ears for a dramatic change of texture. *Verbena* and *Bidens* will add colour, while the grasses and sea holly provide airy height and structure. The grasses, spurges and succulents will continue the display right through the winter.

FOR GROUND COVER
BROAD-LEAVED GLAUCOUS SPURGE
(Euphorbia myrsinites)
Blue trailing stems and acid yellow flowers in summer.

FOR INTERESTING SHAPES AND TEXTURES
TREE HOUSELEEK
(Aeonium 'Zwartkop')
Architectural succulents with rosettes of fleshy, purple leaves. Protect from frost with fleece or overwinter indoors. H: 60cm.

HOUSELEEKS
(Sempervivum spp.*)*
Attractive spiral rosettes of succulent leaves in shades of purple and green.

MEXICAN GEM
(Echeveria elegans)
An easy mat-forming succulent with glaucous green rosettes.

FOR FLOWER AND COLOUR
FERN-LEAVED BEGGAR-TICKS
(Bidens ferulifolia)
Long lax stems with ferny foliage and bright golden daisy blooms in summer. Tender, so grown as an annual.

HARDY GARDEN VERBENA
(Verbena rigida)
Clusters of scented, bright purple flowers in summer.

FOR HEIGHT AND STRUCTURE
QUAKING GRASS
(Briza media)
A tufted evergreen grass with heart-shaped flowers in summer that dry beautifully.

SEA HOLLY
(Eyngium bourgatii 'Picos Blue')*
Spikes of metallic blue around a central cone of flowers.

AN EVERGREEN HANGING GARDEN

Hanging baskets are a brilliant solution when you're short of space, and this multi-layered display gives you even more room to grow. Filled with evergreen plants, it will look great all year round. You can plant up a single species in each layer, or mix it up with different plants that have a range of leaf colours and textures.

YOU WILL NEED:

- A hanging basket bracket or hook (plus a drill to hang it)
- 3 x lengths of galvanised chain
- 3 x hanging baskets
- 3 x matching liners made from sisal or woven coir
- An old compost bag
- Cable ties
- Scissors and metal cutters
- Multipurpose potting compost
- Water-retaining gel and slow-release fertiliser granules
- A selection of evergreen plants

METHOD

Choose where your hanging baskets are to go and attach your hook or basket bracket. Hang the three lengths of galvanised chain from it.

Remove the hanging-basket chains (you won't be using these) and place a liner in each basket.

Decide where the first (highest) basket is to go and attach it to the galvanised chains using cable ties, making sure the chains are evenly spaced around the basket.

Hang the next two baskets, making sure you have enough room for your plants between each one. Count the chain links to help you space them out correctly and keep the baskets balanced. Use scissors and metal cutters to tidy up the cable ties and excess lengths of chain.

To help the compost hold water, cut discs of plastic from the old compost bag and place one in the base of each basket. Fill the basket with compost until it is half full and mix in some fertiliser and gel.

Plant up the top basket first to stop compost falling onto and dirtying the plants below. Then plant up the lower baskets. Water everything in.

WHAT TO PLANT

Any of the compact evergreen plants listed opposite are ideal for your baskets. All will give you lush green growth year round. Some will also add flower and scent. Coral bells come in a range of leaf colours that can be used to coordinate with your other colour schemes, while small ferns, with their long leaves, add architectural interest.

EVERGREENS

Unlike deciduous plants, evergreens have green leaves all year round – they do actually lose their leaves, just not all at the same time.

ELEPHANT'S EARS

Evergreen plants include trees, such as conifers, and lots of flowering shrubs. They hail particularly from tropical and frost-free climates – by contrast, deciduous plants predominantly lose their leaves as an adaptation to cold weather or a wet/dry season.

Being evergreen can also be an adaptation to growing somewhere with poor soil or where the nutrients in the soil are hard to obtain. Plants lose nutrients whenever they lose their leaves, so holding onto them until they age naturally helps them to survive.

CORAL BELLS

PLANT FILE
AN EVERGREEN
HANGING GARDEN

FOLIAGE PLANTS

JAPANESE SEDGE
(Carex oshimensis 'Evergold',
C. oshimensis 'Everest')
Hummocks of green and yellow or
white-striped leaves.

IVY 'IVALACE', IVY 'WHITE WONDER'
(Hedera helix 'Ivalace', *H. helix*
'White Wonder')
The heart-shaped leaves will trail over
and soften the basket edges. Comes in
a whole host of variegated leaf colours.

CORAL BELLS
(Heuchera)
Clumps of ruffled leaves and foliage
in a range of colours. Produces tall
sprays of tiny flowers in early summer.
Look for *Heuchera* 'Obsidian', *Heuchera*
'Marmalade' and *Heuchera* 'Hocus Pocus'.

FERNS

COMMON SPLEENWORT
(Asplenium trichomanes)
A beautiful fern with individual leaflets
dotted along the stems.

COMMON POLYPODY
(Polypodium vulgare)
Pretty, leathery green leaves.

SOFT SHIELD FERN
'PLUMOSOMULTILOBUM'
(Polystichum setiferum
'Plumosomultilobum')
Dense, fluffy fronds form a
cushion of green.

FLOWERING PLANTS

BIG BLUE LILYTURF 'MONEYMAKER'
(Liriope muscari 'Moneymaker')
Lush blade-like leaves and spikes of
violet flowers through late summer and
autumn. Prefers shade.

DARK PURPLE BUGLE
(Ajuga reptans 'Atropurpurea')
Low-growing carpeting plant with purple
leaves and spikes of purple flowers in late
spring and early summer.

ELEPHANT'S EARS
(Bergenia cordifolia 'Baby Doll')
Large, glossy round leaves and sprays of
pale pink flowers in spring.

A POLLINATOR BASKET

Even the smallest container can be of benefit to wildlife and provide you with the thrill of watching it come and go. The key is to grow the plants they love. Pollinating insects, such as bees, butterflies, hoverflies and lacewings, are not fussy whether you grow native or non-native plants – they just want lots of pollen and nectar.

YOU WILL NEED:
- Large hanging basket (40cm in diameter) with liner
- Old large plant pot
- Old plastic potting compost bag
- Multipurpose compost
- A selection of insect-friendly plants – for a 40cm basket, you want 12–15 plants
- Slow-release fertiliser and water-retaining gel
- Bracket or hooks for hanging (plus drill)

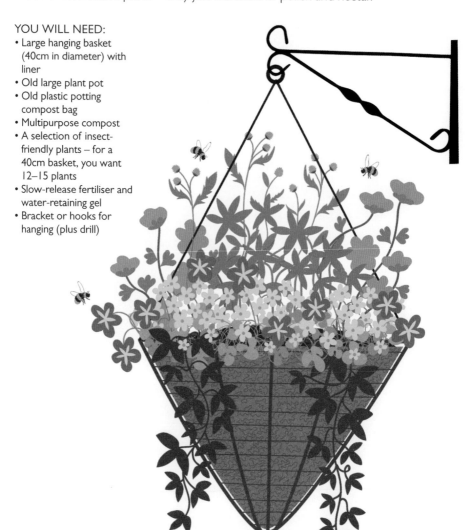

METHOD

Place the liner inside the basket and then stand it in an old plant pot to make planting easier. Cut a disc of plastic from the compost bag and place it in the base of the liner to help hold in water.

Half-fill the basket with compost and then mix in the fertiliser and gel.

Arrange the plants in the basket, placing the larger, upright plants (such as verbena) in the centre and the trailing plants around the sides and edges. When you are happy with the way they look, plant them in, filling in around the plants with compost. Hang your basket on a bracket or hook attached to the wall and water in well.

MAINTENANCE

Deadhead your flowers regularly so that your plants continue to bloom, and feed every couple of weeks in the summer with a high-potash liquid feed, which will also help to promote flowering. Keep an eye on watering and don't let the plants dry out.

The colourful petals of marigolds are attractive for wildlife and are also edible.

PLANT FILE
A POLLINATOR BASKET

Both native and non-native flowers are good for wildlife, but look out for plants with nectar-rich, single flowers, such as *Dahlia* 'Bishop of Llandaff', rather than double blooms, which are harder for pollinators to get into and may not contain any nectar at all. Aim for a broad range of plants for your basket, such as the ones listed here, to achieve as long a season of interest as possible. Plants that flower early and late in the season will prolong the nectar and pollen availability.

LEMON MARIGOLD
(Tagetes tenuifolia 'Golden Gem'*)*
Showy golden-yellow flowers throughout the summer and autumn.

MARIGOLD 'INDIAN PRINCE'
(Calendula officinalis 'Indian Prince'*)*
Deep-orange open flowers.

VERVAIN 'BURGUNDY'
(Verbena 'Burgundy'*)*
A beautiful, rich-coloured trailing verbena that the butterflies love.

TRAILING LOBELIA 'CASCADE SERIES'
(Lobelia erinus 'Cascade Series'*)*
A mass of burgundy, lilac and purple flowers that the bees and hoverflies love.

SWEET ALYSSUM
(Lobularia maritima)
Low growing with white honey-scented flowers that attract tiny beneficial wasps.

TWINSPUR 'ROSE QUEEN'
(Diascia 'Rose Queen'*)*
A mounding plant with rose-pink flowers.

RED CLOVER
(Trifolium rubens 'Red Feather'*)*
Fat spikes of red clover flowers. Great for the bees.

THYME
(Thymus spp.*)*
Tiny fragrant leaves with flowers that are full of nectar for the bees.

RED CLOVER

A POND IN A POT

Water is a beautiful addition to any space, bringing with it movement, texture and, if you're lucky, a buzzing haven for wildlife – insects, such as water beetles and pond skaters, will quickly colonise a new pond, dragonflies will buzz above its surface and birds may well pop by to drink from it.

YOU WILL NEED:

- A large container, such as a barrel, bucket or pot
- Silicone sealant (if necessary)
- A mixture of aquatic plants (see page 88)
- Aquatic baskets
- Aquatic compost
- Gravel or pebbles for top dressing
- Bricks

METHOD

Make sure any holes in the pot are plugged with silicone sealant.

If you can, allow the pond to fill with rainwater. Otherwise, fill it with tap water and then leave to stand for a couple of days before planting to allow chlorine to evaporate.

Before placing in the pond, repot your potted plants into aquatic baskets using a special aquatic compost. Placing pebbles or gravel on top of the compost will stop them floating away.

Lower the plants into the pond, using bricks under the baskets of the marginal plants (those at the water's edge) to get them at the right depth.

Drop floating aquatic plants onto the surface of the water.

MAINTENANCE

At the end of the summer, tidy the pond by clearing away any spent leaves, flowers and stems. As the plants grow, divide and repot them in the spring to stop them getting congested.

SPECIAL EQUIPMENT

Aquatic baskets have latticed sides to allow free water and air movement around the plant roots. Aquatic compost contains a slow-release fertiliser that won't leach nutrients into the water.

WHAT TO PLANT

Look for aquatic plants in the garden centre and aim to get a range of the three main types (outlined below) – at least one of each will help to keep the water healthy and provide a broad range of habitats for your wildlife visitors.

MARGINAL PLANTS inhabit the soil at the water's edge. They are grown in pots with their root ball just below the surface of the water.

AQUATIC PLANT ADAPTATIONS

Aquatic plants grow in water or soil that is permanently wet. Many grow completely underwater or with just their leaves and flowers floating on the surface. Water is denser than air and can support plants really well, so aquatic plants are less firm and stable than land plants, with flexible stems that can move with the water.

Submerged leaves are made up of air-filled cavities and are often long, thin and highly divided, so there is more surface area to absorb carbon dioxide and less resistance to water currents.

Floating leaves are smooth and round with long stalks that can move up and down depending on the level of the water. Some have air pockets for buoyancy.

FLOATING AQUATIC PLANTS have long stems with leaves and flowers that float on the surface. They provide shade (keeping the water cool) and shelter for wildlife.

OXYGENATORS float in the water, producing oxygen and also providing shelter for wildlife.

PLANT FILE
A POND IN A POT

MARGINALS FOR LESS THAN 5CM DEPTH OF WATER

BROOKLIME
(Veronica beccabunga)
Blue and white flowers.

WATER FORGET-ME-NOT
(Myosotis scorpioides)
Blue flowers in late spring.

MARGINALS FOR 5–15 CM DEPTH OF WATER

CORKSCREW RUSH
(Juncus effusus f. spiralis)
Twisted corkscrew stems.

BOG ARUM
(Calla palustris)
Shiny leaves, white flowers in summer followed by scarlet berries in the autumn.

CARDINAL FLOWER
(Lobelia cardinalis)
Scarlet flowers and deep-maroon foliage.

JAPANESE IRIS
(Iris laevigata)
Vivid-blue flowers in summer.

GOLDEN CLUB
(Orontium aquaticum)
Spikes of yellow flowers.

MARGINALS FOR 15–30CM DEPTH OF WATER

LESSER SPEARWORT
(Ranunculus flammula)
Bright-yellow flowers.

ARUM LILY
(Zantedeschia aethiopica)
Fragrant white spathes (flowers) with a striking golden spadix.

BOG ARUM

FOR PONDS 10–30CM DEEP
FRAGRANT WATERLILY
(Nymphaea odorata var. minor)
Fragrant white flowers.

WATER LILY 'PYGMAEA RUBRA')
(Nymphaea 'Pygmaea Rubra')
Pink flowers.

CHINESE WATERLILY
(Nymphaea tetragona)
White flowers.

FOR PONDS 30–45CM DEEP
WATERLILY 'PINK SENSATION'
(Nymphaea 'Pink Sensation')
Pink flowers.

WATERLILY 'AURORA'
(Nymphaea 'Aurora')
Flowers open orange, fading to yellow and then cream.

WATERLILY 'CAROLINIANA NIVEA'
(Nymphaea 'Caroliniana Nivea')
White fragrant flowers.

FLOATING AQUATIC PLANTS
FROGBIT
(Hydrocharis morsus-ranae)
Small white flowers. Plants will sink to the bottom in winter.

WATERLILY
(Nymphaea spp.)
Many varieties available to suit ponds of every size – it is important that you get the right ones for the right depth.

OXYGENATORS (SUBMERGED)
WATER MILFOIL
(Myriophyllum spicatum)
Upright stems with ferny leaves and tiny reddish flowers in summer.

WATER VIOLET
(Hottonia palustris)
Lilac flowers in the summer.

WATER MILFOIL

Waterlily flowers will also benefit insects.

A SCENTED WINDOW BOX

Window boxes may only be small, but they are immediately visible from inside your home so, if filled with beautiful flowers and foliage, they can give you the chance to create your own lush garden view. Add scented plants to the mix, and you can fill the room with a fragrance better than any air freshener. You could change the display with the seasons for fragrance all year round.

YOU WILL NEED:
- Window box or appropriate container for your ledge
- Multipurpose compost
- Scented plants
- Mulch
- Watering can
- Brackets or wire and hooks to secure the box to the ledge or wall

METHOD

Fill the window box two-thirds full of compost, so you can arrange your plants and see what they look like before planting.

Place trailing plants, such as alyssum or rosemary Prostratus Group, along the front so they can tumble over the edge, softening and hiding the box.

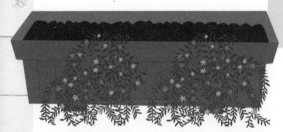

PELARGONIUM

Use large-leaved or eye-catching plants, such as heliotrope and pelargonium, at the ends to draw the eye and make the container appear wider.

SWEET ROCKET

Taller plants should go in the middle of the display to give you privacy – light-textured, airy plants, such as sweet rocket or tobacco plants, will do this but won't spoil your view and still let light in.

Once you are happy with your display, remove the plants from their pots and plant them. Top up and fill in with compost and firm down. Cover with a layer of mulch.

Water the plants in well and then secure your box to the ledge with brackets or wires.

WHY ARE PLANTS SCENTED?

The main reason flowers are fragranced is to attract pollinators, and their fragrance varies depending on the insects that need to be enticed. Most plants smell lovely, but some, such as the striking Dragon arum (*Dracunculus vulgaris*), which is pollinated by flies, smell disgusting – to our noses at least!

Winter flowering plants are often particularly strongly scented. There are so few pollinators around at that time of year that plants, such as

Christmas box (*Sarcococca* spp.), need a strong scent that will travel far to lure as many pollinators in as they can.

Scented leaves are usually for deterring grazing animals from eating them, but in hot climates, such as the Mediterranean, the oil in leaves of plants such as sage or rosemary also stops leaves drying out.

ROSEMARY

PLANT FILE
A SCENTED WINDOW BOX

These plants have an amazing fragrance that will waft into your room on a breeze.

SPRING AND SUMMER
SWEET ROCKET
(Hesperis matronalis)
Mauve scented flowers.

SWEET-SCENTED TOBACCO PLANT
(Nicotiana alata 'Grandiflora')
Delicate creamy-white flowers.

HELIOTROPE 'MIDNIGHT SKY'
(Heliotropium arborescens 'Midnight Sky')
Lovely cherry vanilla scent from rich purple flowers.

BROMPTON STOCK 'DWARF MIXED'
(Matthiola incana 'Dwarf Mixed')
A mix of gloriously scented flowers in late spring.

ANNUAL PHLOX
(Phlox drummondii 'Dwarf Beauty Mixed')
Captivating evening scent and bright, rich colours.

SWEET ALYSSUM
(Lobularia maritima procumbens 'Carpet of Snow')
A continuous mass of white flowers all summer long, perfect for edging and trailing over the ledge.

CHOCOLATE COSMOS
(Cosmos atrosanguineus)
Chocolatey-maroon-coloured, velvety flowers held on delicate stems.

PINK 'MRS SINKINS'
(Dianthus 'Mrs Sinkins')
A classic white pink with an intense fragrance.

SWEET PEA 'PINK CUPID'
(Lathyrus odoratus 'Pink Cupid')
A beautiful dwarf variety with bicoloured pink and white blooms.

PELARGONIUM 'ATTAR OF ROSES'
(Pelargonium 'Attar of Roses')
Rose-scented leaves and pretty bright-pink flowers.

HELIOTROPE

ROSEMARY PROSTRATUS GROUP
(Rosmarinus officinalis Prostratus Group*)*
A spreading form of rosemary with upright spikes of blue flowers and scented dark-green leaves.

AUTUMN AND WINTER

SWEET BOX
(Sarcococca confusa)
Sweetly aromatic white flowers from December to March. Glossy green leaves.

DAPHNE ETERNAL FRAGRANCE
(Daphne x *transatlantica* Eternal Fragrance*)*
Compact semi-evergreen plant, flowers with a delicious heady scent from April to October.

HYACINTH 'DARK DIMENSION', HYACINTH 'WHITE PEARL'
(Hyacinthus orientalis 'Dark Dimension', *H. orientalis* 'White Pearl')*
Plant bulbs in autumn for pungent scent in March and April.

SKIMMIA 'KEW GREEN'
(Skimmia x *confusa* 'Kew Green')*
Dense clusters of scented creamy-white flowers in spring.

WALLFLOWER 'SUGAR RUSH'
(Erysimum 'Sugar Rush')*
Densely fragrant flowers in autumn and spring.

SNOWDROP 'MAGNET'
(Galanthus 'Magnet')*
Honey-scented nodding flowers in late winter and early spring.

A TRAY OF SPEEDY SALADS

Even the smallest windowsill can be productive with a pot of microgreens. Microgreens are simply the seedlings of leafy herbs and vegetable plants that are picked in miniature before they grow any bigger. They are one of the quickest and easiest ways to get fresh edible leaves – most are ready to harvest in just a week!

Most microgreens are grown the same way, in sun or shade, and can be grown inside all year round. Sow a fresh tray every week for a constant supply.

YOU WILL NEED:

- A seed tray, salad box, saucer or any other shallow container
- A fine-textured compost, such as a sieved multipurpose or seed sowing compost
- Microgreen seeds
- Watering can with a fine rose
- Scissors

METHOD

Fill your tray with compost and then firm it down with your hand.

Use your finger to make a series of shallow drills in the compost. They should be about 5cm apart, so you may only have room for two or three rows, depending on the width of your tray.

Sow an evenly spaced row of seeds in each drill – thickly sown seeds can suffer from fungal disease and even fail. Sprinkle compost over them until they are covered.

Water the seeds in gently and place on the windowsill either outside or in, depending on the season.

Leaves should be ready to harvest in about a week – they will take longer in winter than in summer. Use scissors to nip leaves off at the base when they are still small.

WHAT TO PLANT

There is no need to buy specific microgreen mixes – you can use any salad, herb and leafy-green seeds, such as broccoli and kale. Growing these as microgreens is a good way to use up leftover seeds at the end of the season.

Try any of the following:
- Rocket
- Broccoli
- Coriander
- Basil
- Mustard
- Kale
- Fennel
- Radish

PEA SHOOTS

GROWING PEA SHOOTS

These take a little longer to grow than other leaves (between two and three weeks), but are just as rewarding and delicious.

Soak the pea seeds for 24 hours before sowing. Harvest when the shoots are about 5–6cm high by pinching them off just above the lowest leaves. Some may sprout again and give you a second harvest.

VITAMIN BURST

Microgreens aren't just a burst of pungent flavour. They are also packed with goodness.
- Radish leaves are rich in vitamin B6, folic acid and potassium.
- Pea shoots are rich in vitamins C and A, and protein.
- Fennel leaves are high in vitamin C and folic acid.
- Mustard leaves are an excellent source of vitamin K and antioxidants.

A 12-MONTH SALAD POT

In a sheltered, sunny spot you can have your own fresh salad crops all year round. They are quick to grow, with many ready to harvest in just 6 to 8 weeks. If sown in succession (sowing small amounts every couple of weeks), you'll get a constant supply rather than one big glut.

METHOD

Fill the container with compost up to 2cm from the rim and firm it down.

Use your finger or a piece of string to divide the surface of the compost into different sections for each of the crops you are growing.

Sow seeds in each section and water in. Smaller seeds can be scattered thinly along drills made in the soil. Drop larger seeds into holes made with your finger.

YOU WILL NEED:
- Salad seeds
- A large container at least 30cm in diameter and 20cm deep (or a few smaller pots for individual crops)
- Multipurpose compost
- Granular slow-release fertiliser
- Horticultural fleece or cloches

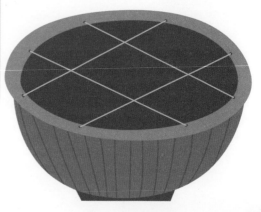

Harvest when crops are ready.

Once a crop is harvested, fork through the compost, sprinkle in a little slow-release fertiliser and sow a new one.

MAINTENANCE

Water plants regularly. Thin out carrots, radishes, spring onions and some beetroot varieties to give them plenty of room to grow. Pick young leaves as soon as they are big enough to eat, using scissors to snip them off at the base. When temperatures start to drop in October, protect plants with a cloche or fleece to prolong harvests through to winter.

PEST PROBLEMS

A common problem for carrots is carrot fly, which drill holes in the roots, making them inedible. Fortunately, they can only fly up to 60cm above the ground, so growing up high on a windowsill or balcony should mean you avoid the problem! However, if you are growing them low down, simply cover plants with fleece.

WHAT TO PLANT

As the seasons change, introduce different crops for a range of tastes and delicious home-grown leaves right through the winter.

CROPS TO SOW IN SPRING

- Lettuce ('Red Salad Bowl', 'Maureen')
- Cut-and-come-again salad mixes ('Speedy Mix', 'Mesclun Mix')
- Carrots ('Adelaide', 'Caracus', 'Mini Finger')
- Beetroot ('Cylindra', 'Pronto', 'Chioggia')
- Spring onions ('Lilia', 'Apache', 'Feast')
- Radish ('Cherry Belle', 'French Breakfast')
- Rocket ('Wildfire')

CROPS TO SOW IN SUMMER

- Beetroot ('Solo', 'Moneta')
- Carrot ('Rainbow', 'Amsterdam Forcing')
- Radish ('Poloneza', 'Amethyst')
- Komatsuna
- Mizuna
- Mibuna
- Winter lettuce ('Winter Gem', 'Winter Density', 'Arctic King')
- Cut-and-come-again salad ('Frilly Mixed', 'Niche Oriental Mixed')

CROPS TO SOW IN EARLY AUTUMN

- Spring onion ('White Lisbon', 'Winter White')
- Mizuna
- Mibuna
- Winter lettuce ('Navara', 'Valdor')
- Rocket
- Lamb's lettuce ('Favor', 'Cavallo')
- Mustard ('Ruby Streaks', 'Red Giant', 'Green Frills')
- Komatsuna
- Oriental green salad mixes ('Stir Fry Mix', 'Bright and Spicy')

A STRAWBERRY PATCH IN A BASKET

Home-grown strawberries are very different from the fruit available in the shops, which are limited in variety and cold-stored, affecting their flavour. They are easy to grow, and their compact, trailing habit makes them perfect for pots and baskets. Growing them in a basket also helps keep them well away from greedy slugs and snails.

YOU WILL NEED:
- A hanging basket and liner
- Waterproof fabric, such as PVC-coated or oil cloth
- A marker pen and scissors
- A knife
- Multipurpose compost
- 6 x strawberry plants
- Straw
- A bracket and drill

METHOD

Draw around the basket liner onto the waterproof fabric and then cut out the circle. Lay the fabric in the basket so that it is evenly positioned all the way round and then puncture a few holes in it with a knife to allow water to flow out.

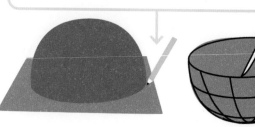

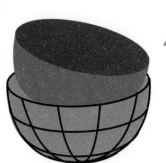

Put the liner on top of the waterproof fabric and then fill two-thirds of the basket with compost.

Space the strawberry plants evenly around the edge of the basket, saving one to go in the centre. Place with the plant's crown at soil level – too deep, and plants will rot; too high, and they will dry out and die. Plant in late summer or early autumn so plants have time to get their roots settled before the winter.

Fill in around the plants with compost, firming it down as you go, and then water the plants in well. Hang your basket in your sunniest, most sheltered spot.

MAINTENANCE

Water plants well, especially in times of drought. When flowers appear, feed plants with a liquid tomato fertiliser every 7 to 10 days. Mulch plants with straw when the first fruits develop to keep them clean and dry, and to conserve water.

Fruits are ripe when they are red all over. Pick at the warmest time of the day for sweet fragrant fruit, and eat straight away. After fruiting, clear away old leaves, stems and fruit to expose crowns to the winter cold and induce a dormant period, which is necessary for the production of new crowns next year.

THE IMPORTANCE OF POLLINATION

Plants that are grown up high on balconies and windowsills may be out of reach or in too windy a spot for pollinating insects to get to them. Do it yourself by rubbing a small brush gently across the stamens in the centre of each flower to transfer pollen from one flower to another.

A WALL GARDEN

Don't waste an inch of space with a vertical wall garden. A simple metal mesh grid attached to the wall and strung with colourful plant-filled pots will transform a dull bare wall into a lush vertical garden.

YOU WILL NEED:
• Mesh metal grid
• Spirit level and pencil
• Brackets
• Drill, masonry bit, rawlplugs and screws
• Plant pots with hooks attached
• Multipurpose potting compost

METHOD

Position your metal grid on the wall, using a spirit level to make sure it's straight.

Mark where the brackets need to go, ideally placing one in each corner and half-way down each side. Drill the holes and attach the grid to the wall with the brackets and screws.

Half fill each pot with compost and then plant up. Fill in with more compost and firm down.

Use the hooks to hang your pots on the mesh grid. Water each pot in well.

MAINTENANCE

Water each pot when it needs it, depending on the type of plant and the conditions of your space, and keep on top of deadheading flowering plants. In summer, the small pots will dry out quickly, so will need regular watering in hot weather.

WHAT TO PLANT

Each pot can contain edibles, ornamentals or a mix of both. Plants can be changed according to the season for a new display every few months, but the following suggestions will provide colour year-round. They are primarily ornamental, with a few herbs to give you fresh tasty leaves whenever you need them. Most of these plants would be best for a bright position. If your wall garden is against a shady wall, thyme will not grow well. Consult the plant files on pages 42–45 for more information on plants for shade.

CORAL BELLS
(x *Heucherella* 'Solar Eclipse')
The scalloped leaves are a stunning mix of deep burgundy edged with lime. Forms dense clumps in a pot and has sprays of white flowers in summer.

BLACK MONDO
(*Ophiopogon planiscapus* 'Nigrescens')
Dark purple-black grass-like leaves. Small purple flowers bloom in summer and are followed by shiny black fruit.

HART'S TONGUE FERN
(*Asplenium scolopendrium*)
A tough evergreen fern with glossy, wavy fronds that mix well with other lacier-leaved ferns.

SEDGE
(*Carex oshimensis* 'Everest')
Clumps of green-and-white striped, grass-like leaves will bring light to the display.

THYME
(*Thymus* 'Siver Posie')
Bushy spreading plants with white-edged fragrant leaves and pretty purple-and-white flowers in late spring.

JAPANESE PAINTED FERN
(*Athyrium niponicum* var. *pictum*)
The deeply cut frilly fronds are grey-green with hints of silver and purple and will arch over the pot edges beautifully.

CHIVES
(*Allium schoenoprasum*)
The edible fresh green leaves provide texture and flavour, while the clusters of bright-pink summer flowers are great for the bees, as well as in salads.

Chapter 4
GARDENING BASICS

Plants can seem to be incredibly finicky, especially when they fail to flower or put on new growth, but they have, in fact, only a few basic needs.

The first step is to grow the right plants for your particular small space, as detailed in the earlier chapters. Then, this chapter will get your small-space garden off to a flying start with information on the equipment you'll need, how to choose the right containers, and how to plant, and how to sow seeds. The technicalities of watering, feeding, pruning and other basic tasks are also detailed here. Things that can go wrong, and how to deal with them when they do, are covered, too.

A quick-reference guide to the necessary tasks of each season helps to get you and your garden in sync with the gardening year, and a glossary decodes some of the horticultural jargon so that your small-space garden can flourish.

WHAT YOU NEED

What you need depends on what you grow, but even just a couple of window boxes will require some basic kit. Investing in a few tools will save you time and make life easier, and you can always expand your kit later on. If you have room for raised beds, a garden fork and spade will make digging and planting easier, and save your back, or if you have more than just a couple of pots, a hosepipe will be useful for making watering a breeze.

ESSENTIAL KIT

HAND TOOLS – a trowel and fork for planting and weeding

WATERING CAN OR HOSEPIPE – one with a fine rose or spray nozzle

SECATEURS AND KITCHEN SCISSORS – essential for pruning and tidying plants

PLANT SUPPORTS – canes, stakes or twigs, trellis, wires and vine eyes for supporting plants and training climbers

GARDEN TWINE – for tying plants to their supports

DUSTPAN AND BRUSH OR A BROOM – for tidying up spilt compost and leaves, and for sweeping the area

BUCKET – for carrying tools, collecting weeds and spent flowers, and mixing compost

CONTAINERS

In spaces without soil, pots and containers will be your essential piece of kit. Almost anything will grow in a pot provided it is big enough, and size and material are far more important than style when it comes to choosing the right pots for your plants.

Always choose as large a pot as you can, as the smaller the container, the more time you will spend watering and feeding your plants. However, do take the weight into account if you have to lug it upstairs to the windowsill or balcony.

New pots come in a whole range of materials and styles, each with its own advantages and drawbacks:

CLAY OR TERRACOTTA

The traditional pot, these are naturally porous, which means they allow air in but water out, so they will dry out in hot weather.

They are also heavy and, therefore, stable, which makes them good for tall or top-heavy plants, but not so great if you need to carry them upstairs or move them. Glazed varieties, which are less porous and frost-proof, are the ones to look out for.

METAL

Metal, including cast iron, stainless steel and copper, makes tough pots that hold water well. However, it heats up in the sun, which can dry out compost, and gets cold in the winter, so pots will need insulating with bubble wrap or newspaper in cold areas. Certain metals, such as lead, can also be heavy.

PLASTIC AND FIBREGLASS

Long-lasting pots that hold water well, these will also be the cheapest pots you'll find. Check drainage holes are adequate, or there at all.

STONE

Some of the most beautiful pots you can buy but also the most expensive. They insulate plants and retain water well, but are heavy to move around.

WOOD

Cheaper, softwood containers are more prone to rotting than those made from hardwood, such as teak or oak, but protect both types with a lining of plastic to make them longer lasting, help regulate temperature and stop wood preservatives leaching into the compost.

OTHER STYLES OF CONTAINER

Make the most of your space and look out for less-traditional container options:
- Hanging baskets are great for flowers but can also be used to grow foliage plants, such as ferns and coral bells, or salad crops and strawberries.
- Pocket planters made of felt, canvas or oil cloth will expand your growing potential and are just the thing for greening walls and fencing.
- Raised beds can be bought as DIY kits, made from wood, recycled plastic or metal, but you can also create your own. They are great if you have a spacious area for gardening, as they enable you to recreate a traditional border and can simply be filled with compost and planted up.

RECYCLING AND UPCYCLING

The great thing about container growing is that just about anything can be turned into a pot, according to your style and budget. Buckets, boxes, sinks and crates can all be recycled and are a lovely way to add personality and style to your space. They are cheap, if not free, and just need a scrub with a brush and soapy water, and some drainage holes made in the base.

MAKING DRAINAGE HOLES

Whatever containers you use, they must have drainage holes in the base so that water can drain freely away and plants don't get waterlogged.

Space the holes across the base several centimetres apart. Use a skewer, scissors, a knife or a hammer and nail to pierce through the base of smaller pots and those made of plastic. For larger pots and wooden, metal or fibreglass pots, first use tape to mark where the holes are to go, then use a drill.

WHAT PLANTS NEED

Your growing space may not be perfect but if you choose the right plants and give them everything they need, you will have a thriving garden. It's up to you to provide them with the soil, food and water that will help them grow, wherever they are.

COMPOST

Always choose the best-quality potting compost. Multipurpose, soil-less composts are the cheaper option and adequate for most plants, but they vary in quality, and most contain peat – if conserving this natural resource is important to you, look for a peat-free alternative.

Soil-based composts are more expensive, but they are good for perennial plants that are in pots for a long time, such as trees and shrubs, because they are heavier and hold on to water and nutrients for longer.

Make sure you use the right compost for the job. For example, use a seed-sowing compost for propagating plants or an ericaceous mix for acid-loving plants, such as camellias.

WATER

All plants grown in containers are dependent on you for water – rain will not be enough – and without it, plants will wilt, weaken and eventually die. Grow plants in the biggest containers you can and check them regularly, pushing a trowel deep into the compost to see if it is moist all the way through. Look out for drooping leaves and stems.

LIGHT

Plants need light to photosynthesise. It's crucial that you choose the right plants for your conditions (see pages 38–63). Avoid overcrowding them and make sure they have enough room to grow without having to compete with each other. Look out for lanky, straggly plants, which may be straining towards the light, and pale or scorched leaves, which may have had too much light.

FOOD

Multipurpose potting compost contains enough nutrients to support your plants for about six weeks, but after that, it is up to you to give them the extra food or fertilisers they need.

Plants require a range of nutrients for good health – some need substantial amounts and others just a trace. The most important nutrients are nitrogen (N) for leafy growth, phosphorus (P) for strong roots and shoot growth and potassium (K) for flowers and fruit.

The amounts of nutrients are detailed on the fertiliser packet in a ratio of N:P:K. General-purpose fertilisers contain a balanced amount of these three nutrients, as well as many of the lesser ones. Fertilisers specifically made for fruiting or flowering are rich in potassium.

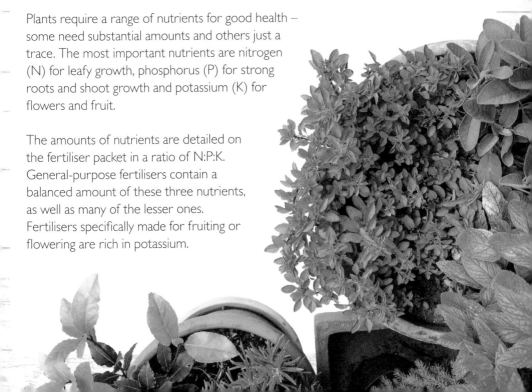

BUYING PLANTS

Plants are available to buy from a wide range of places, from your local supermarket to a specialist online grower. Each outlet has its advantages and disadvantages, but wherever you buy, make sure you are getting strong and healthy plants before you part with your money.

WHERE TO BUY

You can pick up live plants at garden centres, supermarkets, DIY shops, farmers markets and summer fairs. Here you can see the plants, check they're healthy and see exactly what you want before you buy anything. However, stock is often limited, and many shops often only sell plants when they are in flower.

You can also buy plants online or by mail-order catalogue. Although you can't see the plants, this way you have easy access to all the top nurseries from the comfort of your own home. The choice available online is by far the widest.

Specialist nurseries, which tend to grow certain groups of plants such as shade plants or fruit, are the place to go if you are looking for something in particular.

SEEDS, PLUGS OR PLANTS?

The size and type of plants you choose to buy will usually depend on how much space you have and how much time you can spare.

SEED

Sowing plants from seed is by far the cheapest way to start growing. It will give you the greatest choice of varieties and cultivars but is only really possible if you can sow directly outside or have the time, and room indoors, to grow them on.

PLUG PLANTS

Plug plants are mini, sometimes tiny, plants that have been grown on from seed for you to take home and grow on further. Generally available from spring onwards, they are cheaper than larger plants and help you skip the hassle and stress of growing from seed.

CONTAINER PLANTS

There are two types of container plants: 'container-grown', which have been grown in the pots you buy them in; or 'containerised', which have usually been lifted from the ground and planted into pots to sell. Containerised plants are cheaper than container-grown, but only available in the dormant season between November and March.

BARE-ROOT PLANTS

Only for sale in the dormant season and must be planted straight away, these have been lifted from the ground and wrapped in plastic or cloth with no soil around the roots. Opt for fruit trees or bushes, or roses, which are cheaper than potted plants and have a wider choice of varieties.

HOW TO PLANT AND SOW SEED

Whether you're simply growing on plants you've bought from the garden centre or starting salads or flowers from scratch from seed, you need to give your plants the best possible start to help them establish and grow into strong healthy plants.

CONTAINER PLANTS

Established plants can be planted up in containers of your choice, either on their own or in combination with others. Just make sure your pot is big enough to give your plants room to grow.

HOW TO PLANT UP A CONTAINER

Water your new plants and then add potting compost to the container to just below the depth of the plants.

Mix in any grit or slow-release feed now, if needed.

Remove the pots from your plants and tease out the plant roots.

Plant them into the container, adding compost and firming as you go. Leave a 2cm gap between the top of the compost and the container rim to make watering easier.

Water well and mulch (see page 125).

PLUG PLANTS

Depending on their size, plug plants may need to be potted on before they are ready to go into their final pot. Choose a new pot that is big enough for the plug to grow in – 9cm should be sufficient.

HOW TO GROW ON PLUG PLANTS

Stand the plugs in water to soften the root ball and then fill your chosen pot with compost.

Use a pencil or your finger to make a hole, slightly bigger than the plug, in the compost.

Plant the plug gently, firming the compost around it, and then place on a warm, bright windowsill.

Keep them well watered and plant them out once frosts have passed and when roots start to appear at the bottom of the pot.

SEED SOWING

Most seeds can be sown directly into pots outside when the time is right, which is usually in spring when the soil is warm. Before you sow, always check the instructions on the seed packet.

HOW TO SOW SEED DIRECTLY OUTSIDE

Use a hand fork to make sure the compost has no lumps and then water it to help germination.

Use your finger or a dibber to mark out a drill or make individual holes.

Sow pinches of seed thinly along the drill or drop larger seeds into the holes.

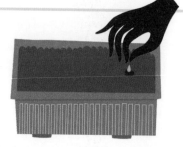

Draw compost over the seeds with your fingers.

Keep the compost moist while seeds germinate.

Thin out the young seedlings to their final spacings, according to the packet instructions.

HOW TO SOW SEED INDOORS

Certain plants need to be sown indoors first, usually because they require a long growing season and so need to be sown early in the year, well before the frosts have passed. These plants include tomatoes, chillies and peppers, aubergines, sweet peas, cosmos and sunflowers.

Fill a small pot or tray with compost and then water.

Scatter small seeds across the compost surface or make a shallow hole and push larger, individual seeds into it. Draw the soil back over the seeds.

Cover the pot with cling film or a plastic bag and seal with a rubber band. Place on a warm, light windowsill and remove the cling film or plastic bag as soon as the seedlings appear.

When the first true leaves appear, transfer the seedlings into larger, individual pots, taking care to handle them by the leaves and not the stem.

Pot on again, a few weeks later, into larger pots. Plant outside once frosts have passed.

UPCYCLED

Any small pot or tray, such as old yoghurt pots, tomato trays or even toilet rolls, can be used to sow seeds in. Just make sure they have drainage holes before you start.

WATERING

All plants need water to survive and, although some moisture is absorbed through their leaves, it mainly comes from the soil or compost they are growing in. Watering will be one of your most important, and demanding, jobs when growing plants, so it is crucial to get it right.

Plants in containers are completely dependent upon gardeners for their water supply, so check them regularly, every day in summer, to see if they need watering. When water is scarce, as it may well be in a spot without a nearby water source, it is also vital to water plants efficiently.

WHEN WATERING, REMEMBER TO DO THE FOLLOWING:

- Use a can with a rose on the end, or a hose with a spray nozzle to make watering easier and more efficient.
- Water in the mornings or evenings, when the sun is low and water will reach the plants roots rather than evaporating. There will also be less chance of leaf scorch at these times.

- Aim water at the roots where it is needed rather than soaking the whole plant.
- Allow the water to soak in as you water, giving it a bit at a time to avoid flooding the plant.
- If compost does become very dry, it can be tricky to rehydrate the plant by watering alone. Submerge the whole container in a bucket of water until the plant perks up.

WATER DOWN TO THE ROOTS

Always water thoroughly – watering too lightly can mean the water just sits at the top of the compost rather sinking down to where plant roots can take it up. Constant light watering encourages roots to grow up to the soil surface to reach the moisture there, which makes them even more vulnerable in dry weather.

WATER SAVING

Water is a valuable resource so try and collect as much rainwater as you can by placing large, open pots or tanks in a space where they can catch it. If possible, divert downpipes and gutters into water butts. Recycling grey water from sinks and baths is also a good way to save water, but make sure you only use eco-friendly soaps and detergents.

IRRIGATION SYSTEMS

If you have lots of pots, have limited time or are often away, an irrigation system is a wise investment that will help both you and your plants. There are a number of different systems available, all designed to distribute water exactly where it's needed, at the base of the plant, and soak the compost gradually, so there is no run off or waste.

Drip-feed irrigation is ideal for watering pots and containers. It is made up of a series of tubes attached to a hose and held in the compost using spikes. Water flows along the hose and is then dripped or sprayed onto the plants.

Use an irrigation system with a hose timer, and plants will get watered automatically. The timer slots in between the tap and the hose and allows you to water at a predetermined time for a certain length of time; for example, for ten minutes every morning.

REDUCING THE NEED FOR WATERING

Remember that plastic pots hold water better than terracotta ones. Soil- and loam-based composts retain water for longer than peat-based ones. Keep on top of the weeds in your pots so plants don't have to compete with them for the moisture in the soil. Grouping pots together will help to create shade and humidity, and reduce the need for water.

MULCHING

Mulch is a thin layer of organic or inorganic material that is spread across the surface of the compost. It is a crucial tool in the battle against drought. It helps to lock moisture in the compost so it cannot evaporate and dry out. It also suppresses weeds, insulates plant roots in the winter and acts as a barrier against pests. Organic mulches will also slowly add nutrients to the compost as they break down.

Get into the habit of applying a layer of mulch every time you plant up a pot. Simply water your new plants in and then scatter a 5cm layer across the entire surface.

Organic mulches include home-made compost, chipped bark and well-rotted animal manure. Inorganic mulches include pebbles and stones, grit, glass chippings, slate and crushed shells.

FEEDING

For plants growing in pots, feeding is as essential as watering. Plants make their own food through photosynthesis and from the soil via their roots. Compost usually only has enough nutrients to feed plants for up to six weeks, so it's up to you to make sure they're replenished regularly after this.

At the planting stage, compost can be given a boost by adding organic matter, such as mushroom compost or well-rotted animal manure, to the mix. Alternatively, there are different types of fertiliser available to add when the plants are in active growth from spring to summer.

TYPES OF FERTILISER

LIQUID FEEDS

Liquid feeds are easy to apply when watering and are 'quick release', giving plants an instant boost, but they do need applying regularly. Common liquid feeds, such as high-potash tomato fertiliser, are applied every couple of weeks throughout the summer months to promote and increase fruiting.

GRANULAR FEEDS

Granular feeds are 'controlled' release to feed plants slowly over time, and are handy and easy to apply. They can be mixed into compost, sprinkled over the top or just pushed under the surface. They are usually added at planting and in the spring to support plants through the growing season.

FOLIAR FEEDS

Foliar feeds are liquid fertilisers diluted and sprayed on leaves, from where plants can absorb nutrients. Most liquid feeds can also be used as a foliar feed. Water over the whole plant rather than just the base, and this will increase the amount of nutrients the plant can absorb.

WORMERIES

It's unlikely you'll have room for a compost heap on your balcony, or generate enough plant material to go in it, but if you have even the tiniest bit of spare space, it's well worth investing in a wormery. A great way to turn kitchen scraps and a small amount of garden waste into nutrient-rich compost and liquid feed, they are available to buy as kits, complete with worms and starter bedding material. Keep it in a sheltered, dry spot and 'feed' your worms as often as you can.

Feed the worms raw and cooked vegetables, fruit, egg shells, coffee grounds, bread, soft green waste, shredded paper and newspapers.

Don't feed the worms onions, garlic, citrus peel, glossy magazines, meat, fish, dairy products, bones or woody plant material.

KEEPING IT GOING

To keep your small-space garden looking its very best all year round, you need to undertake certain jobs at the right time. The spring and summer months are predictably busier than the others, but there is always something to do if you want to carry on gardening throughout the year. Use these simple seasonal planners to advise you what to do when and help you keep on top of the essential seasonal tasks.

SPRING

EARLY SEASON

- Start to sow bedding plants and tender vegetable plants on the windowsill.
- It's planting season – get pots, boxes and baskets planted before the summer to cut down on stress and the need for watering.
- Prick out and pot on plants grown from seed as they develop.
- Plant summer-flowering bulbs.
- Plant up a container pond (see pages 86–88).

MID SPRING

- Quick edibles, such as carrots, beetroot and lettuce, can be sown directly into pots outside.
- Once frosts have passed, sow tender vegetable plants, such as beans and courgettes, directly outside.
- Sow herbs, such as coriander, chives and chervil, outside.
- Plant strawberries outside.
- Nip out weeds when you spot them.
- Be vigilant and on the look out for pest and disease attack.

- Check plants and water when necessary.
- Divide congested herbaceous plants.
- Stake taller plants as they grow to give them support.
- Take cuttings of plants you wish to propagate.
- If necessary, prune Group 1 clematis after flowering, to keep plants in check, and cut back Group 2 clematis (see page 131).
- Give shrubs and herbaceous plants and climbers a general slow-release feed and mulch.
- Mulch all plants to reduce watering and weeding later on.
- Top-dress or repot pot-bound plants and add slow-release fertiliser.
- Put out tanks and water butts to collect rainwater.
- Remove winter insulation from around pots.

SUMMER
....

- Check plants for water every day and look out for pest and disease problems.
- Keep on top of weeds.
- Deadhead flowering plants.
- Tie climbers in to supports as they grow.
- Pinch out the flowers on culinary herbs.
- Take cuttings of plants you wish to propagate.
- Trim topiary.
- Keep sowing speedy veg for a continuous supply.
- Feed fruiting edible plants and summer bedding every couple of weeks with a high potash liquid fertiliser.
- Use netting to protect fruiting plants against the birds.

- Harvest edible plants regularly to keep those crops coming.
- Plant strawberries at the end of the season.
- Put up shade if needed.
- Make arrangements for someone to water your container garden if you are away on holiday.

AUTUMN

- Plant up winter displays.
- Plant new trees and shrubs.
- Plant spring-flowering bulbs.
- Sow hardy annuals and sweet peas on the windowsill for planting out next spring.
- Keep harvesting fruit and vegetable plants until they are spent.
- Plant and sow overwintering onions, broad beans and peas outside.
- Lift summer bedding and spent edible plants and add to your garden waste bin.
- Tidy up plants to stop pests and diseases overwintering. Remove dead leaves and cut back herbaceous perennials that don't have hollow stems or interesting seed heads.

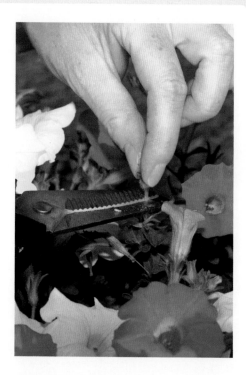

- Mulch container plants with compost or well-rotted manure.
- Bring pots of tender plants inside before the frosts arrive.
  - Cover tender plants with fleece to protect them from the cold and freezing winds.
  - Check climbers are secure before the winter winds arrive.

WINTER

- Cover tender plants with fleece to protect them from the cold and freezing winds, if you haven't already done so.
- Wrap pots in hessian or bubble wrap if freezing weather is forecast.
- Shake any snow from plants to prevent damage.
- Towards the end of the season, start sowing aubergines, tomatoes and chillies on windowsills.
- Chit potatoes.
- Prune deciduous shrubs that require it when dormant, such as roses.
- Cut back all the stems of Group 3 clematis to one or two buds, or 15cm above the ground.
- Plant deciduous trees and shrubs.
- Deadhead and tidy winter displays.

CLEMATIS PRUNING

Clematis are pruned depending on when they flower and are grouped accordingly:

GROUP 1 (Including *C. armandii* and *C. Montana*) flower in winter and early spring on shoots produced the previous summer. They don't need pruning every year but can be cut back after flowering to keep them in check.

GROUP 2 (Including *C.* 'Nelly Moser' and *C. florida* 'Sieboldii') are large-flowered hybrid varieties that bloom from early summer on last year's growth, and are cut back in spring just before they start into growth.

GROUP 3 (Including *C. viticella* and *C. tangutica*) are plants that flower in late summer and autumn, and bloom on the current season's growth. Simply cut all the stems down to one or two buds, about 15cm above the ground, in late winter or early spring.

PROBLEMS AND SOLUTIONS

Unfortunately, some problems with weeds, or pests and diseases are inevitable, no matter what you grow or where. Fortunately, the main offenders are fairly predictable, so keep your eyes open and get them before they take hold.

Good growing techniques will help you have strong, healthy plants that are far less vulnerable to attack from pests and diseases. A healthy plant is a happy plant. Bear in mind the following:

- Always grow the right plant in the right place – it will be happier, healthier and easier to look after.
- Give plants the best start by giving them the best-quality compost.
- Don't overwater or overfeed – too much of either can cause weak, sappy growth that's susceptible to pest and disease attack.
- Don't overplant and overcrowd your pots – always give plants room to grow and develop.
- Find out what pests and diseases might cause you problems and use preventative measures to arm your plants against them.

CHICKWEED

WEEDS

Weeds can ruin the look of your small-space garden, and they will also compete with your plants for food, water, space and light. Vigilance is key. Check your pots regularly so you can spot weeds and get rid of them early, before they have a chance to flower and set seed.

Annual weeds, such as hairy bittercress or chickweed, may only have a short lifecycle, but it's a fast one, often resulting in hundreds of seeds being scattered far and wide. Luckily, they are easy to control – as soon as you see them, just nip them out by hand or cut them off at the base.

Perennial weeds, such as bindweed and dandelions, can be introduced to your growing space as seeds on the wind or in poor-quality green-waste compost. They need to be stamped out quickly. They die back in winter, but will return every spring, and their deep, tenacious roots make them difficult to control. They will regrow if you leave behind even the tiniest bit of root, so dig them up with a hand trowel every time you spot them.

BINDWEED

PESTS

Gardening in a small space should mean you suffer few pest attacks. Those that might reach your growing area may well have been brought in with new plants, so always check purchases carefully. Be vigilant throughout the year to spot pest problems early and keep damage to a minimum.

BIRDS, particularly pigeons, can be a real pest, stealing berries, ripping leaves and stems, and destroying entire young plants. Hang up CDs to scare birds, or use cloches, made from plastic bottles, horticultural fleece or netting, to protect plants.

SLUGS AND SNAILS are a common and frustrating problem for most gardeners, and, unfortunately, there's a chance they may be able to reach your small space. If you spot nibbled leaves and their tell-tale slime trails, look for the culprits on leaves and at the base of plants – night-time is the best time to spot them. If they are a problem, try using upturned citrus skins or saucers of beer to trap them, or secure copper tape around pot rims – it gives them an electric shock and they stay away.

VINE WEEVILS are a problem, both as adults and as larvae. The cream larvae are particularly troublesome for plants grown in pots, and they feed on the roots until plants wilt and, eventually, die. Before you buy a plant, check for any presence of vine weevil by taking them out of the pot and examining the roots.

APHIDS (WHITEFLY, BLACKFLY, GREENFLY) are mainly a problem in spring when there is plenty of the soft new growth they love. They won't kill plants but can weaken them and spread viruses and diseases. The easiest way to deal with them is to encourage their natural predators, such as ladybirds, lacewings and hoverflies, by growing flowering plants. Otherwise, whenever you see them on a plant, rub them off with your hands.

MEALYBUGS are covered in a fluffy white wax that coats leaves. They hide in nooks on plants and are hard to get rid of. Infestations can stunt plant growth. Ladybirds can be used to control the problem, but only in warm temperatures.

DISEASES
The most common diseases of plants grown in pots are fungal and are primarily caused by overcrowding, high humidity and poor air circulation.

POWDERY MILDEW is common in dry weather and appears as a white mould on the upper and lower surfaces of the leaves. To avoid this, keep on top of watering and mulch plants to stop the compost drying out.

DOWNY MILDEW, on the other hand, loves damp, wet weather and causes an unsightly grey fuzz to appear on flowers, fruit and leaves. To keep it at bay, nip off any infected parts and dig up badly affected plants, binning them to stop it spreading further. Avoid over-watering your plants and make sure you water plants at the base rather than over the leaves. Watering in the mornings when it is less humid can also help.

RUST can occur on both ornamental and edible plants and is evident by yellow, orange or brown fungal spots on the undersides of leaves. Remove infected leaves and put them in the bin, rather than adding to the compost heap.

BLACK SPOT is common on roses. It will infect leaves and stems and can stunt plant growth. Black spots can appear on top of the leaves, which can eventually turn yellow and fall off. Collect all fallen leaves to stop plants becoming reinfected next year.

GLOSSARY

ANNUAL
A plant that completes its life cycle (germinating, flowering and dying) in one year.

BARE-ROOT PLANT
A plant that has no, or very little, soil on its roots when purchased.

CLOCHE
A structure, often portable, made of glass or clear material and used to protect plants against cold weather.

CORDON
A means of training a plant, usually fruit trees or bushes, into a single stem with short side-shoots that bear the fruit. Useful for fitting in a lot of plants into a small space.

CROWN
The part of the plant where the roots and stems meet, that sits at soil level.

CULTIVAR
Contraction of 'cultivated variety', also shown as 'cv'. Refers to a plant that originated in cultivation rather than in the wild and is often used interchangeably with the term 'variety' (or 'var.').

CUTTING
A portion of plant material (a shoot, root, bud or leaf) that is cut off and used to propagate a new plant.

DEADHEAD
To remove dead or fading flowers to prevent them from going to seed, promote further flowering and tidy up the plant.

DECIDUOUS
Plants that shed their leaves at the end of the growing season and then renew them the following year.

DIBBER
A hand tool, cylindrical in shape, used to make sowing or planting holes.

EVERGREEN
Plants that retain their leaves all year round and only shed a few older ones at a time (the opposite of deciduous).

GENUS
A category in plant classification that describes a group of closely related plants ranked between family and species.

GROUNDCOVER
Low-growing plants that will quickly cover the soil and suppress weeds.

GREY WATER
Waste water from sinks and baths that is relatively clean and can be reused to water plants.

GROW BAG
A commercial plastic bag filled with nutrient-rich potting compost that is used for growing crops rather than growing them in the ground or in pots.

HERBACEOUS PERENNIAL
A non-woody plant that lives for more than three years and which dies down to the rootstock at the end of the growing season.

HURDLES
A moveable fence panel made of woven hazel or willow.

IRRIGATION SYSTEM
A watering system that provides a controlled supply of water to plants.

LEAF SCORCH
The browning of leaf tissue caused by strong winds, bright sun or drought.

MICROCLIMATE
An area within a garden where the climate or conditions differ from the surrounding area (such as at the base of a south-facing wall).

MICROGREENS
Salad leaves picked when they are just seedlings or very young plants.

MULCH
A layer of material applied to the soil surface to suppress weeds and conserve moisture.

OVER-WINTER
Live through the winter.

PERENNIAL
Any plant that lives for more than two years.

PLANT UP
To transfer a plant into a new, often ornamental, pot.

PLUG PLANTS
Plants bought as young seedlings or plants, and grown on. An alternative to growing plants from seed.

POT-BOUND
A plant that has outgrown its pot. Its roots are restricted, and growth will become stunted.

POTTING ON
To transplant seedlings or young plants into larger pots so they have the room to keep growing.

PRICK OUT
To transfer young seedlings from the pot or tray where they germinated into larger pots so they have room to grow.

PRUNING
The process of cutting back a plant to control its growth, both in terms of size and shape.

RAIN SHADOW
An area of ground next to a wall or fence that is sheltered from prevailing winds and rain, and so receives very little rain.

RAINWATER BUTT
A tank or any container that can collect rainwater when it falls.

REPOTTING
The process of planting a plant grown in a container into a new pot the same size, after reducing the rootball slightly to make room for fresh compost.

ROSE
A perforated nozzle on a watering can that regulates the flow of water.

TENDER
A plant that is vulnerable to damage from frost.

THINNING OUT
The removal of weaker and excess seedlings to allow the remainder to grow to their full potential.

SECATEURS
Garden tools similar to scissors for cutting thicker branches. Popular brands include Felco and Niwaki.

SPATHE
The bract, often white or coloured, that surrounds the spadix in some plants, particularly arums.

SPADIX
A spike of tiny flowers usually enclosed within a spathe.

SPECIES
A category in plant classification, below genus, which describes a specific type of plant.

VINE EYE
A screw with a loop on the end so you can attach garden wire or string to the loop.

WATER RUN-OFF
Excess rainwater that flows across the surface into drains or rivers.

WORMERY
An enclosed system for composting household scraps, which are processed into highly nutritious compost and (depending on the type of system) liquid fertiliser by a community of specialised worms.

FURTHER RESOURCES

The many RHS shows that are held annually across the UK are full of ideas and inspiration. The RHS Summer Urban Garden Show is particularly helpful.

FOR GENERAL GARDENING AND GROWING ADVICE
WEBSITES

The Royal Horticultural Society (RHS)
www.rhs.org.uk

The American Horticultural Society (AHS)
ahsgardening.org

BOOKS

RHS Encyclopedia of Plants and Flowers (fifth edition) by Christopher Brickell (Dorling Kindersley, 2010)

RHS Grow Your Own Crops in Pots by Kay Maguire (Mitchell Beazley, 2013)

RHS What Plant When by Martin Page (Dorling Kindersley, 2011)

RHS What Plant Where Encyclopedia by RHS (Dorling Kindersley, 2013)

FOR SPECIFIC SMALL SPACE INSPIRATION
WEBSITES

The City Planter
www.cityplanter.co.uk

Urban Organic Gardener
www.urbanorganicgardener.com

The Frustrated Gardener
www.frustratedgardener.com

Into Gardens
www.into-gardens.com

BOOKS

The Dry Garden by Beth Chatto (Orion, 2012)

Planting the Dry Shade Garden: The Best Plants for the Toughest Spot in Your Garden by Graham Rice (Timber Press, 2011)

RHS Small Space Handbook: Making the Most of Your Outdoor Space by Andrew Wilson (Mitchell Beazley, 2013)

RHS The Urban Gardener by Matt James (Mitchell Beazley, 2014)

INDEX

IMAGE CREDITS

4 HR-Eleocharis-acicularis.psd
4 © nito | Shutterstock
5 & 25 © Modify260 | iStock
7 © Judith Dzierzawa | Dreamstime
12 © Agenturfotografin | Shutterstock
13 © azure1 | Shutterstock
13 © thirayut | Shuttertsock
14 © Latte Art | Shutterstock
15 © iliart | Shutterstock
15 © Photographee.eu | Shutterstock
16 © martiapunts | Shutterstock
17 © Photodynamx | Dreamstime
17 © Shutova Elena | Shutterstock
10, 18, 19, 111 © Tannjuska | Dreamstime
20 © Tatiana Mihaliova | Shutterstock
21 © Melinda Fawver | Shutterstock
21 © gstalker | Shutterstock
21 © Henri Koskinen | Shutterstock
21 © Olga Lyubkin | Shutterstock
22 © Ifocus | Dreamstime
22 © spline_x | Shutterstock
23 © lulu and isabelle | Shutterstock
24 © steps | iStock
24 © Quang Ho | Shutterstock
25 © neopicture | Shutterstock
26 © Bruce Ellis | Shutterstock
27 © Susan Law Cain | Shutterstock
27 © Atiketta Sangasaeng | Shutterstock
28 © alybaba | Shutterstock
29 © Darkop | Dreamstime
29 © surotbar | Shutterstock
30 © Maria Sidelnikova | Shutterstock
30 © cesaria1 | iStock
31 © Elliotte Rusty Harold | Shutterstock
31 © Lopatin Anton | Shutterstock
32 © pavla | Shutterstock
33 © Darkop | Dreamstime
34 © Naphat_Jorjee | Shutterstock
36 © Franz Peter Rudolf | Shutterstock
36 © Zerbor | Shutterstock
37 © Sandra Knopp | 123rf.com
37 © GarysFRP | iStock
38 © memaggiesa | Shutterstock
38 © Franz Peter Rudolf | Shutterstock
39 © Taweesak Sriwannawit | Shutterstock
39 © martinwimmer | iStock
40 © Michaela Stejskalova | Shutterstock
40 © LorraineHudgins | Shutterstock
41 © rolfik | Shutterstock
41 © TunedIn by Westend61 | Shutterstock
41 © rolfik | Shutterstock
42 © JIANG HONGYAN | Shutterstock
43 © Flegere | Shutterstock
44 © Natalia van D | Shutterstock
45 © Manfred Ruckszio | Shutterstock
46 © Oleksandr Kostiuchenko | Shutterstock
46 © Ingrid Balabanova | Shutterstock
47 © Diana Taliun | Shutterstock

47 © JRP Studio | Shutterstock
47 © Madlen | Shutterstock
47 © spline_x | Shutterstock
49 © Nikolay Kurzenko | Shutterstock
50 © Christine Kuderle | Shutterstock
51 © Richard Griffin | Shutterstock
52 © Ania K | Shutterstock
52 © wasanajai | Shutterstock
53 © Valerio Pardi | Shutterstock
53 © emberiza | Shutterstock
55 © Izabela Edmunds | Shutterstock
56 © Danuta | Shutterstock
57 © SunKids | Shutterstock
58 © lolostock | iStock
59 © litvis | Shutterstock
59 © haru | Shutterstock
59 © Maksym Bondarchuk | Shutterstock
61 © Andrea Jones Images | Alamy Stock
    Photo
62 © Flower Studio | Shutterstock
63 © katyalitvin | Shutterstock
64 © Anfisa Kameneva | Shutterstock
66 © nevodka | Shutterstock
66 © Lifestyle Graphic | Shutterstock
66 © jocic | Shuttertock
66 © Alexandr Vlassyuk | Alamy Stock Photo
67 © azure1 | Shutterstock
68 © Csakanyl | Shutterstock
69 © Michael C. Gray | Shutterstock
69 © wda bravo / Alamy Stock Photo
69 © Barcin | iStock
71 © Tamara Kulikova | Shutterstock
72 © Claudio Giovanni Colombo |
    Dreamstime
73 © piccerella | iStock
73 © forestpath | Shutterstock
74 © photo5963_shutter | Shutterstock
75 © inxti | Shutterstock
75 © Antonio Gravante | Shutterstock
76 © spline_x | Shutterstock
80 © de2marco | Shutterstock
80 © KenWiedemann | iStock
83 © Galushko Sergey | Shutterstock
84 © Elena Koromyslova | Shutterstock
85 © unpict | Shutterstock
88 © Gina Smith | Shutterstock
88 © janniwet | Shutterstock
89 © Tatiana Volgutova | Shutterstock
90 © Manfred Ruckszio | Shutterstock
91 © feawt | Shutterstock
92 72, 128 © Madlen | Shutterstock
93 © HHelene | Shutterstock
93 © Scisetti Alfio | Shutterstock
94 © Kazakov Maksim | Shutterstock
95 © Brandt Bolding | Shutterstock
98 © Ingrid Balabanova | Shutterstock
98 © Elena Elisseeva | Shutterstock
98 © Mariyana M | Shutterstock

99 © Ivan Karpov | Shuttertock
102 © Lamai Kuna | Shutterstock
102 © GAP Photos/Dave Bevan
103 © Nattika | Shutterstock
105 © Oxa | Shutterstock
108 © Hans Geel | Shutterstock
110 © DragonPhotos | Shutterstock
110 © Veronika Synenko | Shutterstock
110 © photka | Shutterstock
111 © Alina Kholopova | Shutterstock
112 © msnobody | Shutterstock
112 © Quang Ho | Shutterstock
112 © Edward Fielding | Shutterstock
112 © Shawn Hempel | Shutterstock
113 © petriartturiasikainen | iStock
114 © Prostock-studio | Shutterstock
114 © Olga Miltsova | Shutterstock
115 © Edward O'Neil | Shutterstock
115 © Mykola N | Shutterstock
116 © scalatore1959 | iStock
117 © Studio-Neosiam | Shutterstock
117 © Richard Griffin | Shutterstock
117 © Maren Winter | Shutterstock
117 © sevenke | Shutterstock
122 © Isa Long | Shutterstock
123 © Hurst Photo | Shutterstock
123 © DESIGNOSAURUS | iStock
124 © DJTaylor | Shutterstock
124 © Frank11 | Shutterstock
125 © Kaipungyai | Shutterstock
125 © mbolina | Shutterstock
126 © winuturn | Shutterstock
126 © Bignai | Dreamstime
127 © Cattlaya Art | Shutterstock
127 © John Glover | Alamy Stock Photo
129 © Anton-Burakov | Shutterstock
129 © merlinpf | iStock
130 © BHamms | Shutterstock
130 © hagit berkovich | Shutterstock
131 © sonia62 | iStock
131 © Le Do | Shutterstock
132 © Franz Peter Rudolf | Shutterstock
133 © jopelka | Shutterstock
133 © Ortis | Shutterstock
133 © suriya silsaksom | iStock
134 © Jiri Hera | Shutterstock
134 © D. Kucharski K. Kucharska | Shutterstock
134 © Evgeny Parushin | Shutterstock
134 © Chalermchai Chamnanyon |
    Shutterstock
135 © Kazakov Maksim | Shutterstock
135 © AJCespedes | Shutterstock
135 © JGade | Shutterstock
135 © Manfred Ruckszio | Shutterstock
139 © RAFFOSAB | Shutterstock
141 © Claus Mikosch | Shutterstock